TALES OF THE AUTISTIC VILLAGE CRICKETER

The frank re-telling of how cricket has given a neurologically 'different' 25-year-old the chance to fully experience life!

By
Josh Williamson

First published in Great Britain by Fine Leg Publishing
finelegpub@gmail.com

Front cover image by Josh Williamson
Back cover sketch by Elly-Ann Williamson (Ravenmaiiart)

All photographs were taken by the author or permission has been given by the copyright holders

EDITED BY Jools Pattinson, Dave Williamson and Carl Taylor

PRINT ISBN: 978-1-8382035-1-1
E-BOOK ISBN: 978-1-8382035-0-4

CONTENTS

CHAPTER FOUR:
LIFE IN THE 20'S (THE BILLY YEARS) : 2015 - 2019

EPILOGUE
QUOTES AND ACKNOWLEDGEMENTS

FOREWORD

Hello, you may not have heard of me, but my name is Josh, and although I am not a professional cricketer, or anywhere near that ilk of prestige; I am a high functioning autistic person and want to share with you my cricketing life, and all the significant events surrounding my involvement with this great sport. Looking back, maybe it was fate that cricket has been my lifelong passion; after all, my impending birth was announced at Viv Richard's final game on English soil in 1993 at Canterbury! This said, I feel it is necessary at this age of 25, that to create a tangible manuscript of my life relating to the single most important entity within it, would be an enlightening, inspiring and timeless thing to do. So that whatever offspring I may produce in the future and for generations further down the Williamson line knows of me, Josh Williamson, and how I became the man I am today.

Admittedly, what you are about to read is a slow burner; it starts sedately but I hope the laughs and enjoyment that you get from reading this, is equal to myself writing it! In this series of real-life cricketing stories under the central theme of cricket, it explores how autism has impacted my life, how I developed from a socially awkward youth, to an adult who isn't much different. But how my issues have, for better or worse, had some rather comical happenings during my near two-decade tenure of playing amateur cricket. Fundamentally, the sole reason I am penning these memoirs is purely for my love of cricket and everything that playing the game has allowed me to do in my life. Most of the memoirs are funny; many situated in inebriated circumstances later down the line! A few sad, and several I hope, inspiring for anyone with autism that life does indeed understand you, and that most things don't go above your head like everyone thinks. Whoever you might be; you are talented, life is worth living, but most importantly, when you have found your niche in life, it is truly amazing!

This book will begin from when I started playing cricket at the age of nine in 2003, and finish in the year 2019; aged 25. Clearly, not every story is situated on the cricket field, but rest assured, every account in this comprehensive catalogue of true-life events has solely occurred because I play cricket, and many – because I'm autistic! This index of true tales will take you from the early days as a Thanet under 10's unorthodox leg-spinner; to tours, cricket weeks, and stag-dos with my close mates that were exclusively made through the communal enjoyment and love of playing the game. So sit back; relax, and digest each memoir as its only little piece of the lengthy and complex puzzle that is the cricketing life of me, Josh Williamson; the Autistic Village Cricketer.

PROLOGUE

With Billy, one of my best mates, just about successful in his mission to meet myself and Carl on time to watch the first ball of day three at Lord's; we eventually found ourselves waiting at the home of cricket's gates. It was here where I started to show the typical signs of someone with my condition; it was busy and we were packed liked sardines to enable our entry into the ground. I was quite literally sweating like a pig in an abattoir! Bill saw this so he reminded me that I do have an ASD card for situations just like this, and suggested that I show it to a guard and gain entry via a side gate.

"Great!" I thought. *"I won't have to wait in this crowded line much longer!"*

Having said that, although our unenviable state of 'fish in a tin' wasn't helpful, the excess quantity of perspiration omitting from my hairy armpits probably wasn't helped by the addition of a smuggled bottle of red wine in my bag! Now, for those of you that don't know. Lord's is the only professional ground in the world where for international cricket fixtures, they allow one bottle of wine to be carried into the ground for personal consumption. With us clearly intending to be there all day, one bottle of wine would simply not be enough to last the duration! I needed extra supplies!

Knowing full well an eagle-eyed Lord's steward would inspect every nook and cranny of my rucksack before allowing us to even walk into the sacred ground; the day before I had preempted this eventuality.

"What did I do? I hear you ask. "How did you hide the bottle?" Well, in the lead up to our trip to the capital, by deciding to hide this bottle of red wine, I didn't just mask this thing with a jumper or something more ordinary! Oh no! It was intricately packed within a hollowed-out French stick, pretending to be my lunch! It didn't quite fit around the entire bottle though. So, in a genius display of creativity, my mother then conjured up the idea to wrap the wider bottom half in a thick layer of tin foil. Where in 'garnishing' this liquid luncheon disguise, she then dressed the top with the most limpest bit of wet lettuce she could find! To be honest, what she orchestrated that day could have even fooled the Enigma machine! Anyway, I think this was why I was panicking so much, as essentially I was like the wine variant of a Pablo Escobar drug maul!

The preliminary ticket checker of course allowed me to walk through the side gate, where I soon found myself in front of the bag checker. After I hauled the overly-heavy rucksack over my shoulder and unintentionally slammed it onto the trestle table, it made this most noticeable 'tink' sound. I thought to myself;

"Oh God! You must have heard that! If you ask one question it will be curtains for us watching any cricket today!"

I say 'curtains', as anyone who is aware of the difficulties people with autism can face, they tend to be terrible at lying! Any question, innocent or likewise, would have meant giving the game away and that guilty 'tink' probably just sealed my fate! So, there I was, slowly opening the zip in the optimistic hope that he didn't care, and would simply wave me though to my seat in the stands. After taking an inordinately long time to reveal the contents, the guard grabbed his torch and didn't utter a word as he started digging for any fermented contraband! With the sweat now dripping off my youthful brow, he looked in the left corner; nothing. He glanced towards the right; he looked towards the right again! Where he instantly darted his attention up towards my ever-increasingly worried self!

"Shit!" I thought. *"He knows! I'm probably going to get banned from Lord's for life!"*

The guard subsequently inhaled a large gulp of air to signify he was about to say something where he... **To be continued.**

CHAPTER ONE:

HOW THE CRICKET FASCINATION BEGAN : 2003 - 2004

HOW IT ALL BEGAN! - 2003

C ricket. It's a funny game isn't it? It's funny how one chooses to spend every Saturday afternoon in the summer playing a sport, only to entertain the possibility that your sole involvement might be getting a golden duck and touching the ball twice in 40 overs! It's funny how cricket can even be called a sport! When in fact every week, without fail, you eat a tea plate that's comparable in height to Mount Snowdon! But isn't it funny that even though I'm only 25, how one seemingly inconsequential event can lead to a lifetime of character defining moments. This - is the story of how it all began!

Being a 90's baby, in 2003 I was nine years of age. It was a great year; England won the Rugby World Cup, Arnold Schwarzenegger became the Governor of California, and Marcus Trescothick hit his highest test score of 219 vs South Africa in the last test of the summer! As such, this is where my cricket story begins, on a mildly-warm summer's day in early September, sitting in front of a silver 32" CRT that was about as thick as ten TVs' made in

2019; watching that majestic innings from the left-handed genius with my father and grandpa. Everything about that inspirational; amateur-career-starting innings was full of free-flowing cuts, pulls and extra cover drives, that when witnessed, it would make anyone want to start playing the game for themselves! So, that's exactly what I did, I confidently asked my mother to book me on to the next cricket coaching course as soon as possible! However, due to the presence of a notoriously slow dial-up internet connection at the time, it did take her a while to source something, but eventually she scouted a block of ten winter softball Saturday morning sessions; I couldn't sleep for a month I was that excited!

So, the time finally came; the first Saturday in October arrived! I hopped out of bed, trundled downstairs where it was here that proudly Dad gifted me his very own 'first bat'; a 1968 Stuart Surridge. It was very worn, so much so that even the bottom corner was perished due to his own childhood crease tapping in the playground! I was insistent that we left the house unnecessarily early to ensure we arrived on time, where I was soon greeted by two kind and ageing coaches; Graham and Ian Dovey. Graham, a softly spoken man, and Ian, a softly spoken northern man. Both seemed really happy to have me there! This was until they started the first session. Having at the time undiagnosed ADHD and autism, it was imperative their sessions were fun and engaging, when they weren't, trouble would soon ensue! Consequently, I was clearly soon attributed with the label of the 'naughty kid', but this didn't stop Ian and Graham from coaching me the game that I initially found so fascinating. In fact, the opposite was true, due to my clear natural ability to play the game, they persevered in equipping me with the fundamental knowledge and skills within all three disciplines to become competent in the art of playing cricket. As the weeks elapsed, due to my strong understanding of rules and procedures, by the end of the forth Saturday session, I had worked out the best method to most effectively score runs in the adapted quick cricket game. Because of the rule that all one was required to do to score runs, was to make contact with the ball, I surmised that if I could master the art of the 'forward defence', I could a score heaps of runs every week while also negating the possibility of getting bowled or caught. This angered all the other children as I could spend a large amount of time batting! It actually got to the point that I felt like a bit of a cricket superstar as all the other kids knew who I was; who was a benefit to their side because of this innate ability to flawlessly replicate that ever dependable shot, time after time.

STAT ATTACK: THE SCHOOL TUTOR ORDEAL - 2004

After these introductory sessions, we fast forward to the spring of 2004. England were touring the West Indies, and Brian Lara was at his peak! Building upon Trescothick's inspiring 2003 innings, this is where the genuine enchantment of the sport blossomed; the statistics! This was only encouraged by Lara's record-breaking 400 not out at St-John's in Antigua! To apply a pertinent metaphor; Cricket is like Cocaine to drug addicts to people with autism, and this record-breaking innings established that addiction. To this day, I keep a beautifully organised spreadsheet with my own runs, wickets and wicketkeeping stats so I can analyse my personal figures at the end of each season. This obsession got to the point in April of 2004, where I would even set up some stumps on my one-square-foot upstairs landing at home, so I could create scenarios and scorecards from this series. I even made a fake game where England overcame the follow-on, and set a score to win the Test match to best Brian Lara's 400 not out!

This interest of cricket statistics endured when my mother forced me to attend a school tutor to support my lacking English and Maths skills. This partnership with that lady; however, did not stand the test of time, as it only lasted five weeks! Having said that, during this time, the only method in which this tutor could get me to actively engage with her pointless tutorials was via implementing scorecards into her teaching pedagogy. I insisted upon this stimulus for a month, even though every week ended in tears due to her nagging and monotonous teaching style, telling her to Foxtrot Oscar too many times to count! Even though this ended badly, the initial draw of trying to write match reports and analyse professional cricketers' stats, was enough to bring about this subjectively unhealthy attachment to cricket!

CHAPTER TWO:

JUNIOR SUCCESS! : 2004 - 2008

BREAKING ON TO THE THANET CRICKET SCENE - 2004

After the school tutor ordeal, the winter sessions worked to good effect as this next memoir is situated in the summer of 2004. I was, somehow, selected for the Thanet District under 10s; Ian Robinson is now my coach. As part of the pre-season squad sessions, it was found that in addition to my supernatural ability to protect my wicket, I was sighted by Ian as to my, 'indifferent' approach to bowling leg spin. I say 'indifferent', as I held the ball like an off break bowler but rotated my wrist in such a way that it created the necessary lateral movement off the pitch to be strangely effective. It was a slow start to selection into the main XI, but just like in the English test team, when a drop-out occurred, I took my chance! So, on a sunny day in June vs St-Lawrence College, I returned bowling figures of 2-0-8-2. I essentially became, 'un-droppable'! In that short spell, Ian witnessed the immaculate line and length of each delivery, he observed the perfect flight that utterly deceived their number seven batsman, but most importantly, he saw the unwavering passion and determination to succeed in such a young boy! This belief in my unorthodox leg spin bowling abilities was supported by my follow-up appearance vs the Dover district. Again, in a similar fashion to the first game vs St-Lawrence, I returned figures of 4-0-5-3! I distinctly remember that if I didn't get a wicket on a delivery, I would get frustrated to the point that Ian needed to take me to one side and remind me that I can't get a wicket every ball, otherwise the game wouldn't be very long! These successful spells in the 2004 Thanet under 10s team was rewarded by, again, my analysis of the end of season statistics. With a season's bowling average of 4.40, and along with it, the best bowling average in the team! I was top of the tree! To this day this is one of my many claims to fame, that I had a better bowling average than Ian's son, Ollie, who is now playing professional cricket for Sussex and currently the proud owner of over 200 First class wickets!

The 2004 unorthodox leg-spin bowling grip

Bowling Averages 2004

Bowler	Overs	Maidens	Runs	Wickets	Best Bowling	R.P.O	Average
J. Williamson	10	4	22	5	3-4	2.20	4.40
O. Robinson	19	3	43	6	3-3	2.26	7.17
R.	13.4	5	46	5	3-0	3.37	9.20
J.	12	1	68	5	2-15	5.67	13.60
A.	17	0	69	4	2-10	4.06	17.25
K.	30	3	133	7	2-12	4.43	19.00
J. Dewell	15	0	66	2	1-5	4.40	33.00
Also Bowled:							
M	3	1	9	1			
K.	5	0	27	1			
T.	9	2	32	0			
K. Asiedu	8	0	30	0			
R.	1	0	4	0			
J.	1	0	6	0			
L.	1	0	8	0			

MARGATE EARLY DAYS: THE CREATION OF QUIRKS - 2005

This sudden storming of the Thanet youth cricket scene in 2004 produced a more fulfilling reward in the spring of 2005. A letter fell through the post box one April morning, it was an acceptance letter from Ian; the Thanet under 10s coach. It said that I had been selected to play for the Margate under 11s 'A' side! This was a time unheard of by children today; every club in Thanet had two junior sides in each of the age groups of Under 11's, 13's and 15's, so making it into the side that didn't lose a game in 2004, for me, was a real accomplishment! It wasn't all smelling of roses for myself though! I excitingly arrived for my first training session of that season, expecting to reproduce the magic of the year prior, but when I bowled my first delivery in the nets, I couldn't get the ball straight and bounced it three times! I was rather embarrassed to say the least! My persistence to replicate that charmed leg spin was to no avail for the first fortnight of the 2005 season; it appeared I had got the yips! I soon came to realise this, and came to the emphatic conclusion that if I were to tweak the ball with my fingers in the form of an off break bowler, and give it enough flight to land on the moon, batsmen of my age would not be able to resist the temptation to over hit their shots and walk past the ball when attempting to turn my 'pies' into easy scoring half-volleys. This variety of effective wicket-taking bowling brought forth my very first cricket 'quirk' in regard to playing this great game. Before every delivery was launched into the stratosphere, my brain compelled me to do two things: sniff the ball to make sure it's the same ball and attempt to pass wind to ensure I don't accidentally expel any gas when sending up the next Apollo mission! This act of smelling the ball was quickly picked up by my teammates, which I'm sure many people with autism have to endure; subsequently mocked. However, this creation of my first playing 'quirk' was quickly embraced among my peers, and swiftly celebrated as an advantageous method in obtaining wickets for my team!

The summer of 2005 was; however, a somewhat quiet year in terms of cricketing accomplishments. This was the year a MCC tradition started though; it was the beginning of the augural Margate cricket club junior tour! This was arranged by Ian every year for about four or five years where we travelled as a team to East-Anglia in Norfolk and Suffolk. Every year, 12 boys', the same age as myself, were supervised by Ian and my dad, to take on the best junior sides in the minor cricketing counties. This was also the year we were all given a tour cap, which not to spoil too much, I still have this hat and play in it to this day! However, moving slightly on to the latter years of the tour, the 12 of us would be split up into two groups to occupy two apartments at Pontins. There were four bedrooms in each dwelling, each sharing a room and an adult chaperone in their own bedroom. Great fun was had every year and really helped solidify my love of the game! It's just such a shame that these memory forming tours could probably could never happen today and help secure a love of cricket for the next generation!

THE CATCH OF THE CENTURY - 2006

A fter a season establishing myself as a reliable member of the successful junior side, one Sunday afternoon in 2006 I was invited to make up the numbers in what would be my debut adult fixture. I could not tell you who the opposition was, who else played, or even the date. All I can recall is that it was at home and dad roped me in to make up the eleven.

Being a 12-year-old at the time of this game, I was not expecting to be positioned anywhere in the field where I could be required to regularly stop a firmly struck cricket ball. This expectation; however, did not come to pass. From the first over of the game, the captain in his infinite wisdom designated that my starting fielding position would be at backward point. This did not get off to the best of starts! A few overs elapsed without my inexperienced intervention, but then to my unknowing surprise, a thick outside edge came somewhat sedately along the floor towards my general vicinity! I knew exactly what I needed to do; left knee down, right knee bent, and both hands covering the small gap between my legs to stop the ball.

Otherwise known as the long-barrier. Although this theory was sound, the application of such a simple and universally recognised cricketing manoeuvre was not quite so comprehensive! Before I knew it, the ball simply trickled through my inadequately positioned legs and limped towards the short boundary behind me. The look of astonishment from the bowler, that I had actually missed the ball and caused four additional runs to his figures, was as if I had decapitated his cat! He did not look pleased. However though, he understood that I was only 12, and was participating in my first adult game, so this look did not last long.

It was only two overs later, when the same batsman that was gifted a boundary through my incompetent fielding abilities moments earlier, was back on strike facing the same bowler and clearly eyeing up this 12-year-old boy for more easy runs. This, ultimately, was his downfall. So, there I was, still withholding belief from our captain that I couldn't possibly make the same mistake a second time, and, smack! With the full clout of a 3-pound trunk of willow, the opener performed an immaculately timed backward-cut that clearly had no intention of staying down! So, just like a salmon in a freshwater river, I flung the full weight of my chubby body from the standing sedentary position towards the ball using my weaker left hand, and just like an insect in a venus fly trap, the ball somehow wedged itself firmly in between my small child-sized fingers. I was amazed!

The bowler couldn't believe it after witnessing the events two overs prior, but most importantly, the batsman had to make that lengthy trek from the bottom of the square back to the clubhouse, knowing full well that a 12-year-old fat boy pulled off the catch of the century! It was especially funny at tea, when I attempted to collect his personal thoughts on that piece of individual fielding brilliance. All he could retort was, *"You lucky bugger"* and replicate his deathly stare from earlier. I simply chuckled, shuffled along the crowded tea line, and picked up yet another cheese and pickle sandwich...

Looking back at it now, how that full-size cricket ball ever remained in my hand is a complete and utter mystery, but all I know is that it made my presence known to the entirety of Margate cricket club, and firmly set me up for a long and illustrious amateur cricket career.

THE STRIDING INCIDENT - 2006

Continuing the 2006 theme. In that year's junior tour, we stayed in a selection of chalets directly adjacent to the Norfolk broads. For whatever reason, that year my family decided to attend this cricketing excursion to the county, where the team stayed in two chalets and my family in a separate cabin. I obviously elected to stay with my family due to a more cushty living arrangement of my own room, as well as the familiar structures and set personal routines. However, one evening I meandered over to one of the team's chalets to participate in some of the organised entertainment. Little did I know what the future had in store for me on that fateful night!

To provide some necessary context, during the week of the 'Norfolk Broads Tour', Cameron instigated a little known practical joke of 'striding' his fellow teammates. For those of you that don't know what that is, this is a prank when someone unknowingly pulls your trousers or shorts down in public to eventual embarrassment for the victim. Anyway, halfway through this character-building evening, Cameron caught a larger than expected handful of my somewhat 'loose around the waist' trouser leg, where he was able to effortlessly swipe off, not just my ill-fitting tracksuit bottoms, but unfortunately for me, my underwear as well! Being only 12 in 2006, unfortunately puberty hadn't been so favourable in gifting me a pre-pubescent 'shower', and very much in the vein of a youthful 'grower'. So much so, that everyone present was compelled to take a second look. I don't know how or why this was never brought up again in future social gatherings as I have grown up, but I'm rather grateful that day was never spoken again until now! Nevertheless, I have since overcome this early poor hand by Mother Nature to curate a well distinguished post-prepubescent identity, and am rather proud to narrate that this somewhat embarrassing childhood chronicle.

'Got Headache!' - 2006

The striding incidents didn't end there however! Oh no! Although Cameron's perpetual obsession of pulling someone's trousers that year was all fun and games with the lads, there is another tale! On the same 2006 tour, Cameron's mother elected to join the team to enjoy some well-earned rest and relaxation. This however never materialised! In conjunction with having to spend a week with six teenage boys' in a chalet, Cameron's striding spree was most indiscriminate in choosing his victims! One evening, while a group of the boys' were participating in board games to pass the time one rainy evening, Cameron's mum appeared at the door threshold to inform everyone as to when dinner would be ready. Cameron, not playing the time filling games, snuck up behind his mother, and as quick as a flash, proceeded to reposition her shorts around her ankles! Fortunately, unlike me, her over-sized white granny panties remained firmly in place, but she went absolutely crazy! Shouting at her son,

"This tour, all you've done is give me a headache!"

To which, while banging his palm across his temple, Cameron sarcastically replied in what can only be the most realistic impersonation of 'Sloth' from the Goonies;

"Got headache!"

The look of her unwavering stare and expression on her face was of a woman scorned, she evidently was not amused! As far as I can remember, she even prohibited him from playing the rest of the tour!

THE KENT CUP WINNING RUN - 2007

The year is now 2007, my pies and stone wall batting technique are starting to attain a somewhat legendary status within the Thanet cricket community, and spoilers, Margate under 13's won the Kent Twenty20 cup! To ensure this tale isn't as long as a PhD thesis, under the management of Ian and the captaincy of his son, Ollie, we categorically had the best team in the local area; whereby, from my memory, we didn't lose a game against a Thanet based team for the tenure of my junior cricket career!

So, in a year where our dominion of the local teams incited only demoralisation and a perceived hatred for the sport from our opponents, we proceeded to enter the Kent Twenty20 knockout cup. To save you the finer details, Margate expectantly sailed past the Thanet district stage, bested the quarter and semi-finalists with relative ease; meeting Adlington CC in the final at the Mote county ground! This was an enthralling fixture where both sides showed a real desire to be the best in the county! It seemed however, as if Margate wanted that prestigious title a fraction more; winning the game and making our their way to the south-east of England playoff!

In the draw, we were awarded an away game vs Reigate CC; in Surrey on the 22nd July; 10:30am start! We thought that as we had to make such a long journey at sparrows fart, we didn't stand a chance of winning! So, in an attempt to intimidate Reigate, we rocked up an hour before and implemented a series of warmup drills to give the perception that we were a quality junior outfit. It clearly worked to good effect! After winning the toss, we elected to insert the opposition to have a bat and set us a score to chase. It initially seemed that our decision was a poor one as Kris and Jamie Dewell both opened up the bowling; conceding 40 runs. Reigate's racing start was however soon halted where Kris was able to dislodge four scalps for not too many! We thought they were about to crumble; but like all well equipped teams, Reigate had other ideas. After a slight resurgence in their batting endeavours, and the apparent liking of our resident leg-spinner Ellison, who in this situation went for an expensive 17 in his two overs. Our captain, Ollie, wisely caught my attention and gave me the nod. I couldn't help but think -

"Shit! There's two set batsmen at the crease; my hands are clammy; I'm going to cost us the game!"

As it happened, I should have had more belief in myself! I calmly collected my thoughts, smelled the ball, tried to fart and casually meandered into the bowling stride of my first delivery. I threw up one of those all too familiar grenades; however, unlike my ever-dependable offerings that land on a 50p piece, it was a waist-high full-toss! Clearly, the pressure had got to me much like our primary leg-spinner; however, the batsman failed to capitalise on this early Christmas gift, and proceeded to present me with my birthday and Xmas presents all in one; by slapping the ball directly to Ollie at deep square leg! Like they say, shit really does get wickets! This piece of fortune somewhat settled my nerves and returned some sufficiently tidy figures of 2-0-9-2; including the scalps of those counter-attacking lower order batsman I was so concerned about earlier. In the end, abetted by my pie-shaped tributes and due to a great team effort; Reigate only scored 86 from their 20 overs.

On re-entering the changing rooms, it was felt this would be the easiest run chase in history, and pending any collapse, we'd be making our way to the south of England finals in Horsham. Clearly though, the fact I reminisce this tale, it was not. After a start where we were cruising; swiftly finding ourselves 60-4 from ten overs, we felt we couldn't lose! Reigate, again, had alternative thoughts on the contrary! After being in such a strong position, the wickets soon began to tumble. Kwaku was out for a duck; five down. Jamie managing a modest seven runs; six dismissed. Ellison — out for another duck; seven back in the pavilion. Emma made a solitary run; eight gone. I know! We even had a girl playing! How very 21st century! Anyway, at this point, along with some supplementary extras, we limped our way to 84-8 from 18 overs. With both myself and my best childhood mate; Dan Weaver at the crease. We both knew full well that another wicket would only mean inevitable failure, due to the hopeless bunny at number 11. Dan, clearly showing signs of crippling nerves on the last ball of the 19th over was somehow able to wrangle one down to third man, which facilitated a scampered two. It is now 86-8 from 19 overs. Two wickets from Reigate, it would be a bowl-off, or one run to win it here and now! Being at the striker's end, I was completely out of my comfort zone, not only did I have the weight of the entire team on my shoulders, I wasn't able to drop and run the necessary single for victory, as all the fielders were in protecting that possible outcome. I was surrounded with nowhere to go and was unable to replicate my favourite shot I so comprehensively learned four years prior. I distinctly remember not knowing where I was going to hit the ball as the bowler ran in, but if memory serves me right, he assisted in my thought process by firing down a pitched-up delivery; outside my off stump. With nowhere to run, I had to go, 'over the top'. Fortunately for me, the field was so close, any connection with the ball would be sufficient. So, with this away-swinging delivery hurtling towards me, I latched on to the leather with what was probably the bottom-most part of the toe, and unconvincingly looped the ball over the cover fielder! I suppose, if Reigate had a conventional field, it probably would have nestled nicely into the catcher's hands; only one wicket away from an unlikely tie. However, as it was, all they could do was watch and take in the sight of this chubby, long-haired, tail-end blocking specialist confront their opening bowler to realise south-east glory!

In the Newspaper after Hitting the Winning Runs

Another title: Margate Under 13s are the new South-East England champions.

Star men: Josh "Monty" Williamson and Dan Weaver, who were at the crease when Margate scored the winning runs.

Margate are best in the south-east as well

Horsham Finals Day: The Great Spike Heist! - 2007

With not much time to relish on our historic win vs Reigate, we only had a week to recuperate our essential energies before the trip down to Horsham to play in the south of England finals. Much like in the professional county T20 area, semi finals and a final were due to be played on the same day, to ultimately have the opportunity to represent the region in the whole of England playoffs! On the first day of the school summer holidays, we turned up ready and raring to play the local finalists; Hastings Priory CC. After success in our decision to bowl first in the last knockout tie, our skipper Ollie elected to bowl first again, which, like last time, was intended to place the onus of pressure on the opposition. If memory serves me right, Ollie decided to open the bowling with his immaculately flighted off spinners, which meant I was not required to recite my faithful rendition of sending projectiles over a figurative World War One trench. This policy worked to good effect; restricting Hastings to a gettable 91-9 from their 20 overs. We learned from our endeavours in the previous round to not take this run chase for granted. So, in what seemed customary fashion for the Margate under 13s, we steadily made our way to 43-3 off the first ten with both Kris and Ollie still at the crease. Only needing 48 from the second half of our allocated overs, we all thought the game was surely in the bag! Then — tragedy hit! In the space of an over,

Ollie was run out attempting to complete a three when clearly only two was on offer, and Kris? He was comprehensively and emphatically skittled. With just five wickets left and only myself, Jamie, Dan and Ellison who could reliably stick around, what proceeded was a mission too far for Margate under 13s, as we could only muster 78 out of the required 92.

We clapped off the eventual finals day winners, and was promptly directed towards the pavilion for luncheon. As I was a not out batsman in our futile pursuit, I clearly was still wearing all my gear when the remainder of the team had changed into something more comfortable. To retract slightly from this tale, due to my at the time undiagnosed neurological developmental incompetencies, I had an issue with taking my shoes off in unfamiliar locations. This childhood mental block on the removal of such items of clothing reared its awkward head at Horsham. Upon arrival at the entrance of the pavilion, a steward divulged the strict rule that spikes were not permitted indoors. This clearly was an issue for a defiant 13-year-old Josh, as the only way one could acquire their sausage, beans and mash lunch was by walking over to the other side of the large room stepping on loud, hard-wooden flooring.

As the act of walking over to the prepared buffet-style lunch forced you to walk past the tables where all four teams were positioned, I thought to myself that if I could sneak entry into the pavilion, walk on the heels of my spikes directly to the tables and sit down immediately, I could get away with keeping my shoes on! And this is exactly what I did! To not cause detection of my cunning plan, before entry, I pushed past a few of my teammates to ensure I was hidden in the middle of the line, I precariously balanced my top-heavy frame on the heels of my feet and quickly made my way to the end seat of Margate's pre-assigned dining table. However, the unfortunate outcome of this 'great spike heist' resulted in two things. One; I didn't have any lunch, and consequently caused great discomfort and hunger, and two. The fact this 13 stone, 13 year-old-boy had no food, even though it was free, caused nothing but perpetual questioning and suspicion from teammates, coaches and kitchen staff alike! I clearly couldn't say anything as this would have given the game away, where my only rationale for a lack of midday sustenance was,

"I'm not hungry, I'm too angry to eat, we should have won".

I thought the gig was surely up! No one could have possibly believed these outrageous falsehoods! I was just about to confess my heinous crimes, when, Ian stood up and said,

"Right boys, are we ready for some fielding catches before the third and fourth place playoff?"

I was overwhelmingly relieved; the plan had worked! I consequently stood up and cautiously repeated the 'balancing on heels act' and made my way out of there unscathed from any potential teenage humiliation!

Ok, I must acknowledge that I didn't get any lunch in this convoluted defiance of rules, but Mum had some bits leftover from her pre-prepared Marks and Spencer's picnic! I just couldn't entertain the thought of wearing socks in the pavilion. The most important thing was that my ASD compulsions were satisfied, and I could enjoy the losers playoff game in psychological peace! From memory, even though we lost that game as well, Ian let me open the batting, where I believe I batted 12 of the 20 overs for about 12 runs! This all said though, when I look back at that day, what happened doesn't really matter, we all had a great time and were still the best in Kent and the south-east of England!

DON'T MESS WITH THE PIE MAN! - 2007

This series of tales continues the run of 2007 memorable stories in the form of that year's junior tour to Norfolk. After the eventful cup run and ultimate loss to the hands of Hastings, this tour with four friendly fixtures arranged, arrived rather punctually. Before I delve into the specifics of that year's infamous tour, it is safe to say that personally, I had a good time of it! Glossing over the boring bits, accumulatively in the 2007 Norfolk tour, I returned home with 14 scalps at an average of 6.35. There are a number of highlights included in this collection, including the hat trick versus Brook CC; however, this doesn't top the chart of recallable stories. That honour goes to the spell of bowling and subsequent feedback from the opposition in the final game against Lowestoft.

We arrived on a blustery, but pleasant Friday in the middle of August. Upon the decision after the uncontested toss to bat first, we were informed that half the Lowestoft under 13's also played for the age group's minor county. In retrospect, as I write this tale, I have serious doubts as to the accuracy of that claim, but such is life! As previously said in an earlier memoir, we had 12 lads' play on these tours, and as such, due to a couple of somewhat lengthy innings from myself on the Tuesday and Thursday, I was asked by Ian to sit out from the batting lineup but take the field to reproduce the wizardry seen vs Brook. I cannot for the life of me remember what we scored in the first innings, but it was something to bowl at. After the statutory opening overs from Kris and Jamie, and the fruitless spells from the 1st change bowlers, it was soon my time to replicate my comprehensive re-enactment of trench warfare! As I strolled towards my mark at the beach end, Ollie lobbed me the ball to take any whiff of victory away! I thought to myself,

> *"I already have ten wickets in three games, let's make a bit of Margate cricket club history and get 15!"*

So, as customary, in my bowling ritual, I once again sniffed the ball, tried to fart and walk into my delivery stride. With a little lateral tweak, and enough flight to amass snow on the seam, the first victim didn't have a clue! It seemed the batsman played about five different shots by the time the ball plummeted onto the necessary length! By which time, he found himself advanced about five feet down the pitch and indecisive in his shot selection. Eventually, he chose to play a shot with such a colossal amount of intended force that one could only describe it as an 'agricultural masterclass'. Clearly, connection was not made and Sam, in typical fashion, artfully dislodged a solitary bail. Hysterics ensued; Sam had his all too familiar grin on his face, Ollie gave me that knowing look of - *"Oh no! Here we go again"*, and Kris supplemented this with his typical jibe to the effect of -

"How has this happened? This should never be allowed; why can't it be me?"

The rest of the spell felt like groundhog day. The recurring batsman's nightmare repeated itself a further three times, to the tune of four wickets for only six runs! In conjunction with the earlier wickets in Lowestoft's run chase, the damage was unquestionably inflicted when my four overs had concluded. I was able to relish the remaining overs of the tour and walk off the pitch in the proud knowledge that we had won every game of that year's tour supported by my personal bowling performances.

Well, that is how I wanted this fairy tale to end. The reality was that I led the team off the field, held the ball high to signify a respectable bowling performance, and all I could hear was a barrage of insults from the half minor county opposition.

"How did he get four wickets!"

"He's so shit, he couldn't get my nan out!"

"What an absolute disgrace!"

In an unusual occurrence, where normally I was a stuttering wreck, I wielded the uncharacteristic witty retort of;

"Well, if I can't get your nans' out, you all must be worse than a 70-year-old woman!"

That clearly didn't bode well for the team to partake in the traditional after cricket socialising. So, as quick as a flash, Ian hastily ushered the 12 of us, and my dad, towards the minibus to make a swift and expedient departure back to Margate and bring forth the end of the 2007 junior tour!

The 2007 Tour Averages

Complete Player Summary

All matches, Norfolk Tour, Margate Cricket Club 06-Aug-2007 to 31-Aug-2007

#	Name	Club	Mts	Inn	NO	HS	50	100	Avg	Runs	Ovs	RunsA	BBowl	5I	10	Avg	Wkt	Ct	St	RO
1	J Dewell	MCC	5	4	-	3	-	-	1.50	6	10	55	1-2	-	-	13.75	4	3	-	-
2	B	MCC	5	4	3	59*	-	-	169.0	169	14	53	2-9	-	-	17.66	3	1	-	-
3	A	MCC	5	4	1	34	-	-	25.00	75	8	46	2-6	-	-	23.00	2	3	-	1
4	R	MCC	5	4	-	71	1	-	33.25	133	5	27	1-9	-	-	13.50	2	3	-	1
5	S	MCC	5	2	1	5*	-	-	10.00	10	12	57	5-12	1	-	7.12	8	1	-	-
6	K	MCC	5	5	2	63	1	-	41.66	125	7	41	2-10	-	-	20.50	2	2	-	-
7	T Padiachey	MCC	5	4	2	50*	1	-	50.50	101	9	75	2-19	-	-	25.00	3	2	-	-
8	D Padiachey	MCC	5	3	1	10	-	-	8.50	17	14	52	3-10	-	-	13.00	4	-	-	-
9	O Robinson	MCC	4	5	2	52	1	-	43.33	130	12	53	3-12	-	-	17.66	3	-	-	-
10	D Weaver	MCC	5	2	-	2	-	-	1.00	2	16	86	1-21	-	-	43.00	2	2	-	1
11	J Williamson	MCC	5	4	2	33	-	-	32.50	65	18	89	4-6	-	-	6.35	14	1	-	-
12	S Winch	MCC	5	4	1	50*	1	-	31.00	93	1	14	0-14	-	-	0.00	-	4	-	-

CREDIT CRUNCH TOURS - 2008

After the great tour of 2007; the following year was slightly less prosperous. In what would be my last season as a junior, for whatever reason, we went on two back-to-back tours in Norfolk and Cornwall, in what would also be our final excursions as the famous 'Margate Invincible's'. The decision to instigate two tours back in 2008, was an apparent odd one, because as we all know, due to the affluent financial bankers, 2008 was the start of a long recession. However, none the less, all our parents backed our cricketing abilities and determination to play junior amateur cricket and paid for us all to go! So, once again, we turned up outside the rickety metal gates of Tivoli Meadow, packed our bags onto the back of the minibus and hit the road for our last hurrah! Although the events of the Norfolk tour are acutely rather foggy, the 2nd tour to Cornwall is far more well defined. The reason for this somewhat poorly timed scheduled trip was simply so as an under 15's team we could try and win both the under 17's and 15's Cornwall club tournament!

This endeavour went so smoothly initially on the first day of play, competing in an adapted floodlit 3G football ground, whereas a team we bested our U17 opposition with relative ease! This process continued into the second day, until the rain hit! For the entirety of that day, after winning the only playable game in the morning, we sat inside; huddled around a 20-inch CRT and enjoyed our own competition of Gran Turismo Three! Being the team from Margate and myself having poor awareness of social cues, this meant that even if opposition teams tried to gain possession of the wired PS2 controllers, I was there to blindly overlook all senses of 3rd party frustration, and load up yet another three-lap race with my ever faithful Ford Mustang in camel brown and red racing stripes!

Eventually, the rain relinquished its perpetual deluge on the Cornwall club's cricket square, where it was time to play. Although, again, I continue this theme of forgetting the finer intricacies of the actual cricket in this tournament, I do remember three things in sequential order. One; in the game that followed, after the never-ending PlayStation rain delay, I bruised the entire inside of my right palm in pursuit of warming up my already loose fingers. Two; I then didn't play for the entirety of that day, and the fixtures the day after because of this. And three; because I felt entitled to play in the U17 final, over and above of one of the player's brothers' who was only 11, this meant I bruised my hand even more in attempt to prove my fitness to Ian!

So anyway, the day of U17's final came around, as a group of barely under 15's, life was smug, and I had a fitness test to pass! I'm not sure Ian was particularly fussed whether I played or not, but there we were on the side of the ground with Kris hitting a ball as hard as he could to prove my un-readiness to participate. This; however, was simply a mind over matter situation and as the game only lasted 20 overs, I never gave into his over enthusiastic attempts to prove otherwise, and hence took the field to take home glory.

From memory, we batted first in this all too familiar event of playing in finals, we most certainly got a competitive score to defend. It was going so well, until it abruptly came to me at deep extra cover. The batsman, three years my senior, lifted the ball over the fielding ring but softly enough to force an amazing piece of work to send him packing. That amazing piece of work didn't quite materialise. I completed the hard work of running in and making the required ground; however, as I pounced forward to pouch an unlikely snag, the ball simply rebounded out of my right hand and nestled nicely on the dew-laden grass. Ollie didn't look pleased; Ian had this head in his hands, and unsurprisingly, Kris had that all too familiar smug look on his face that plagued my entire junior cricket career. We went on to lose that final but win the under 15's competition. From memory, we were awarded with a large haul of kit, most of which was utter rubbish, but I did get a new lid out of it!

Anyway, in celebration of a job well done. Ian took the executive decision to blood this group of 14-year-olds in the way of a 'curry night'. Little to his knowledge, I, just like many other autistic people, are very fussy when it comes to food and nutrition. Curry consequently was included in that category of 'fussy'. So, off we went in the minibus to the nearest Tandoori, where we were swiftly provided with a menu and the statutory poppadoms. I thought -

"Oh lovely, a massive crisp like thing with mango jerry and yoghurt, maybe this Indian food isn't so bad!"

Oh, how I was wrong, I drew my attention over to another table in the restaurant and was not too keen on the look of this type of culinary phenomenon. So, when it came time to ordering our food and drinks, three things were ordered: chicken nuggets, chips and a becks blue! I know I know, you must all be thinking, the 14- year-old fat boy must love his chips and deep-fried chicken; however, that look on the waiter's face was as if this had never been ordered before in his restaurant. It must be noted that experience of the mint yoghurt on poppadoms was enough for one day, curry in a Tandoori was a step too far in a single bout for this autistic boy!

CHAPTER THREE:

AN AUTISTIC COLT MISINTERPRETING AN ADULT WORLD : 2009 - 2014

THE FIRST FIFTY: WHAT A PALAVER! - 2009

As we transition from junior cricket tales into stories of the open-age adult game, I begin this chapter with a memoir that, although historic, leaves a slightly sour aftertaste as I reminisce upon the events of my first-ever fifty on a sunny August day in 2009.

This day is so firmly attached within my memory, I shall remember it until the day I die. One Sunday in the middle of August, the Margate Sunday 2nd XI ventured down to Snodland, near Maidstone, to play Lloyds CC. As was customary with such a young side selected to play, in Mum's green Vauxhall Zafira, we were required to meet at Tivoli Meadow beforehand to ensure we arrived at the venue with a full side. From memory, taking transit with us was a certain young, fresh-faced Dan Carter playing in one of his first ever adult fixtures. Anyway, we arrived in good time, gave the pitch its obligatory assessment; whereby the skipper on the day, our 75-year-old groundsman; Mick Bush, came to the executive decision that it was a not dissimilar to a Falklands minefield and un-apprehensively inserted the opposition into bat.

It was a good start from Lloyds vs our youthful Margate team; whereby, they some quick runs to put them into the driving seat. Being the captain and the oldest representative in our team, Mick elected it was prudent to also keep wicket. Being a man of considerable vintage in 2009, it must be noted that somewhat due to this decision and our lacking experience as a team, a few byes and dropped catches whistled past his perished keeping apparel, which ultimately facilitated a fairly defendable target of 184 in 40 overs.

As we ambled off the pitch to enjoy our well-earned mid-innings refreshments, Mick walked next to me, placed his fingers on his cancer affected throat cavity, and uttered a batting number in his unforgettable gravelly textured voice. *"Three?"*, he expectedly requests, to which I unequivocally felt obliged to accept. Knowing my fate in the 2nd innings batting order, this resulted in a 'small' amount of food on my tea plate to ensure I was in peak physical condition to successfully fulfil my now fateful batting endeavours. If memory serves me right, I stacked: seven sandwich triangles with an assortment of fillings; four homemade flapjacks; a bag of prawn cocktail walkers; both halves of a scone with strawberry jam and cream;

controversial I know, but strawberry jam first! And a banana to contribute to my recommended 'five-a-day' requirements!

Our reply to Lloyd's 184 didn't start well, as my junior comrade Jamie, was out with only nine on the scoreboard. So, there I was sat a little too comfortably wearing my pads in this foldable blue bucket camping seat, when Jamie spooned one in the air! I was absolutely nowhere near ready to make my way the crease, primarily on account that I was still finishing the last of my four homemade flapjacks when I was forced to hurriedly wipe the last sweet crumb from the corner of my gluttonous mouth; position my lid and gloves on, and take wield of my GM Icon 808! Still with the lingering taste of raw onion and 'oaty' sweetness from the tea that I only just finished consuming two minutes earlier; I wandered out to the middle, fist bumped the outgoing opener, gave words of condolence for his lost wicket; and proceeded to pat the war zone that someone had the audacity to call a cricket pitch! I looked up to our umpire and politely requested a guard of middle; I scratched my mark the statutory four times before setting myself for what I regard as the most memorable innings of my life! As always, I was little nervous, but what came first was something that could be construed as a 'nerve settler'. The opening bowler stormed in; clearly full of confidence after his first, and spoilers, only scalp of the day! Where he delivered this juicy 4th stump half-volley, which I was only too happy to help myself to; obtaining the reward of four runs and a one-ball strike rate of 400!

This start; however, did not continue. In tried and tested fashion, as always following a boundary, the first thought that went through my mind;

> *"Keep your head down Josh, nothing silly, block the next ball".*

This happened on all occasions in this innings whenever a boundary was struck; however, not everything was smooth sailing. Soon after my entry to the crease, Vivek's departure inevitably ensued. With the score now 33-2 and Mick encouraged by my current efforts; he made his own way to the popping crease to try and replicate what he had witnessed in the five overs prior. It was an enlightening experience in my first, and only, batting partnership with Mr Bush. In his ten runs from 37 balls, I can recount three times I nearly got run out! But the real tale here was my confession between overs of an inability to play a particular medium pace bowler, and the explosions he was detonating on the minefield. I, somehow, was able to see off an over from this chap; however, when in a further conversation with Mick between overs I stated this ever-fateful string of 'uncalculated' words;

> *"I don't want to face this bowler, he's going to get me out! Can you face him?"*

The look on Mick's face was as if I had disgraced and urinated on his dog's grave! There consequently were a few 'choice' words used by him before he was most un-ceremonially castled by the very bowler I distilled grave innings ending reservations about! He subsequently stormed off the pitch; called me a word that begins in 'C' and rhymes with 'hunt'; throwing his bat by the boundary side in unequivocal disgust in the process!

Being only on 30 at the time and knowing that not too many recognised batsmen were to follow, I knew I had to see the side home and complete the previously unattainable dream of fifty runs. What followed could have only been regarded as a 'batting masterclass' by everyone apart from the skipper, whom in his opinion caused his downfall. The innings had it all; back foot extra cover punches; leg side clips off the pads to guarantee strike rotation; and booming shots straight over the top off the spinners! I believe my only perceived blemish was a top edge that went for six to the short deep square leg boundary! Fortunately for me, the boundary was only a 30-meter swipe, so I think I got away with it!

That six took me on to 47, one more hefty blow and the maiden half century was mine! As was expected, the next ball I unsurprisingly patted back to the bowler, and then, smash! I shuffled down the track via a little skip in the knowledge that my performance up till that point was faultless, and consequently made crisp connection with the ball to hit it over mid-on for a one-bounce four! The childhood dream I first envisaged when I watched Marcus Trescothick six years prior had finally come to materialisation! The lid came off as quickly as the trousers of a virgin the first time they have sexual intercourse; the bat held high and hugs came about a little too liberally! I, Josh Williamson, had scored a half century!

The victory in the game; however, was not yet mine. I thought to myself, if we lose this game my first batting milestone will all be in agonising vein; I needed to push on! With 80 still required from the final 15 overs, the game was by no means a foregone conclusion. So, in partnership with Dhesh and Pete, who also played a pivotal role in our run chase, accumulating 34 and 14 respectively, we moved the score swiftly along to 172-5 when Dhesh holed out. With myself still in and cruising the ship towards a categoric and emphatic win; disaster struck! Taking a little too much for granted, my first mistake of the entire innings would also my last! I followed in Jamie's footsteps and spooned the ball to mid-on! I was out for 80 from 103 balls in 150 minutes. The game was still not won! We still needed six runs to win, with only four wickets remaining, all of whom were self-confessed hopeless number 11s with a nosebleed, due to the unavoidable altitude sickness as they all can't bat 11! My first and only thought was of complete and utter dread! If we lost the game from here, I would never hear the end of it from Mick! Luckily, Pete was able to crash a beautiful cover drive to the boundary to bring home the win!

I walked on the pitch that day a gluttonous 15-year-old boy who liked flapjacks a little too much, and walked off it a hero—who still liked flapjacks a little too much! The deafening display of applause and kind words followed as I retreated back to the pavilion was truly unforgettable! All apart from one man; Mick. He refused to even look at me and say well done. All I received was that same look of disgust and resentment I experienced an hour and a half earlier. Even though I single handily won us the game with some added assistance, he was unable to rescind his previously spiteful behaviour and allow a boy to savour and relish in his first individual batting milestone.

The days that followed were of sheer, unequivocal delight. As Dad scored the game electronically and was able to create a wagon wheel of where I had scored my runs! I insisted Mum drive us to see Grandpa at his care home; Maurice House. So I could provide him with a ball by ball, run by run analysis of the innings. I couldn't sleep for nights due to a perpetual mental imprint of the shots within my 80. Which as you can imagine, when I didn't get the text to play in the following week's fixture, I was utterly demoralised. Mick, a 75-year-old RAF veteran was being a vindictive 'so and so'. Mum rightly stormed right up to the club chairman at the time, and demanded Mick be stripped of his captaincy because of the way he responded to my reasonable request; that himself, a senior player, face a particular bowler due to a 15-year-old's inability to play him.

And that's exactly what happened, he captained his final game that Sunday, and if memory serves me right, also played his final game as well.

This being told, I don't however wish to talk ill of the dead. After this little episode of Mick's self-indulgent captaincy, He and I actually became quite good friends in the years following. Where after an interluding frosty period in the subsequent months and early portion of the 2010 season. After a dodgy-looking 40 in a pre-season friendly, we mutually agreed that in retrospect, the whole palaver most certainly made me a better cricketer in the long run! We would often laugh about what happened; talk about general game tactics; current affairs in the cricketing world and most interestingly, his days within the RAF. My life was most definitely enriched after listening to his wealth of experiences and vast insights into his past and the sport that we both hold so dear!

Rest in Peace Mick.

The Wagon Wheel to the Momentous Innings

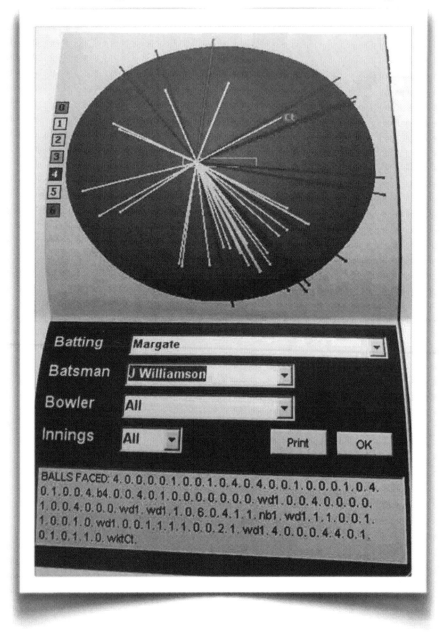

Batting   Margate

Batsman   J Williamson

Bowler   All

Innings   All   Print   OK

BALLS FACED: 4.0.0.0.0.1.0.0.1.0.4.0.4.0.0.1.0.0.0.1.0.4.
0.1.0.0.4.b4.0.0.4.0.1.0.0.0.0.0.0.0.wd1.0.0.4.0.0.0.0.
1.0.0.4.0.0.0.wd1.wd1.1.0.6.0.4.1.1.nb1.wd1.1.1.0.0.1.
1.0.0.1.0.wd1.0.0.1.1.1.1.0.0.2.1.wd1.4.0.0.0.4.4.0.1.
0.1.0.1.1.0.wktCt.

The Scorecard to that Memorable Game

MATCH SUMMARY				
MATCH:	Lloyds vs. Margate	DATE(S):		15 Aug 2009
VENUE:	Lloyds Snodland	TOSS WON BY:		Margate
CAPTAINS:	S Green	(Home)	M Bush	(Opposition)
WICKETKEEPERS:	E Hultson	(Home)	M Bush	(Opposition)
UMPIRES:	Not Recorded, Not Recorded	RESULT:		Margate won by 4 wickets
SCORERS:	Dave Williamson, Not Recorded			

1ST INNINGS

BATTING TEAM: Lloyds								1st INNINGS
Batsman	How Out	Bowler	Runs	Mins	Balls	4's	6's	FOW
S Green (c)	lbw	A Richford	34	43	38	5	0	115 for 5
C Walker	lbw	J Dewell	14	52	45	1	0	54 for 2
A Read	bowled	J Williamson	33	44	37	6	0	177 for 7
R Read	not out		4	4	2	1	0	
N Young	c R Dellaway	P Shakeshaft	18	30	26	3	0	39 for 1
E Hultson (w)	c & b	M Patrick	7	13	16	1	0	65 for 3
L Hultson	bowled	A Richford	5	3	3	1	0	177 for 8
P Lutman	bowled	D Padiarchey	13	77	53	1	0	115 for 4
A Melville	not out		1	0	2	0	0	
C Green	bowled	A Richford	0	3	2	0	0	183 for 9
D Blackmore	c M Patrick	J Williamson	15	38	25	2	0	170 for 6
Extras	b: 21 lb: 3 nb: 2 w: 14		40	p: 0				
		TOTAL:	184	WKT: 9		Overs: 40.0		

BATTING TEAM: Margate								1st INNINGS
Batsman	How Out	Bowler	Runs	Mins	Balls	4's	6's	FOW
V Shama	bowled	L Hultson	12	26	20	0	1	33 for 2
J Dewell	c N Young	A Read	5	8	8	1	0	9 for 1
J Williamson	c S Green	C Green	80	150	103	12	1	179 for 6
M Bush(c)(w)	bowled	L Hultson	10	36	37	1	0	65 for 3
J Magee	c E Hultson	A Melville	11	34	34	2	0	102 for 4
D Padiarchey	c A Read	C Green	34	48	39	4	0	172 for 5
P Shakeshaft	not out		14	9	9	3	0	
D Carter	not out		0	4	2	0	0	
A Richford	Did not bat		0	0	0	0	0	
R Dellaway	Did not bat		0	0	0	0	0	
M Patrick	Did not bat		0	0	0	0	0	
Extras	b: 4 lb: 1 nb: 1 w: 15		21	p: 0				
		TOTAL:	186	WKT: 6		Overs: 39.3		

BOWLING TEAM: Margate				1ST INNINGS		
Bowler	O	M	R	Wk	NB	Wd
P Shakeshaft	6.0	2	19	1	1	0
J Magee	4.0	1	17	0	0	1
M Patrick	8.0	1	24	1	0	2
J Dewell	4.0	1	5	1	0	1
D Padiarchey	7.0	0	26	1	1	0
V Shama	3.0	0	19	0	0	0
A Richford	6.0	0	34	3	0	2
J Williamson	2.0	0	16	2	0	3

BOWLING TEAM: Lloyds				1ST INNINGS		
Bowler	O	M	R	Wk	NB	Wd
A Read	8.0	0	22	1	0	0
L Hultson	8.0	0	38	2	0	2
C Green	8.0	2	21	2	0	1
A Melville	6.0	0	30	1	0	4
S Green	4.0	0	24	0	1	5
C Walker	1.0	0	11	0	0	1
P Lutman	4.3	0	37	0	0	2

THE WICKET-KEEPING INHERITANCE - 2011

After the 2009 batting heroics and the subsequent maiden fifty, the following year was a little dry in terms of runs for a teenager struggling to find their feet in playing solely adult cricket. Sadly, 2011 was also the year my grandpa, Peter Clarke, died at a very reasonable innings of 90. The only fifty he was alive for, was my first. This was the man I always went straight to when achieving anything special when playing, the man who counselled me to create my initial batting technique; how to hold the bat, stand at the crease and the why it's so important to defend my wicket like it's my own life. The man who sparked my fascination and nurtured my love of the game; had died.

After a triumphant war with leukaemia ten years prior, where he was only ever days away from dying for months. In the April of 2011, Grandpa fought and, tragically, lost a short second battle. This being told, I'm not a religious man or even a spiritual being, but I often glance back at that fact. Because this man battled so bravely in 2001, he was able to enjoy, not only another 10 years of life, but watch his only cricket-playing grandson reach the age of 16; not six! I do not doubt that without my grandpa's borrowed decade, I unquestionably would not be the cricket enthusiast I am today, and undoubtably would not have any of these memoirs to write!

Not to turn this tale into a retrospective eulogy, but for the context of what I'm about to describe, this is of the most utter importance. Back before and after World War Two, Grandpa played for Dartford CC; where he kept wicket and opened the batting. Because of his apparent success within his own playing days and perhaps, due to his membership of the MCC, the Hoppers Tie Club (*which I have been a member of since turning 21*) and Kent CCC, he not only crossed paths with some legends of cricket but made good life long friends with them. To quite evidently name drop a few stars of Kent and English cricket: Bob Wilson, Colin Cowdrey and Derek Underwood would be naming only a few. He was such good friends with Bob, that his and Marlene's (Bob's wife) daughters' grew up alongside Mum; whereby, we are all still good friends today! Maybe it was fate that one of their daughters; Julie and her ex-husband Steve Marsh; are my Godparents! Even though I understand Steve was playing in a Sunday League fixture vs Derbyshire on the 21st of August, so apparently Bob actually stood in at the baptismal font!

Anyway, growing up, Grandpa would always tell me of the days when he played and how he pointed his bat towards gully but would always bring it down straight to play the ball. Although he would always make these memories perfectly apparent, he would never coerce me to specialise in any particular discipline.

However, after these regular discussions, I do think he secretly wanted me to become a wicketkeeper! Unfortunately, as a developing cricketer in my youth, I never took yield of these conversations; only taking the opportunity to try my hand at it within a game in 2010. Needless to say, that first time I was appalling! I mean — I was terrible! Dropping multiple catches and even missed an opportunity one would could only define as 'regulation'! Keeping never again, definitely crossed my mind.

So, there I was in May of 2011, a month after Grandpa's death; still in the process of mourning him, when we were due to play Macknade CC in a Sunday fixture. With us not possessing our usual wicketkeeper in the available XI; our skipper, Kash, requested one or two volunteers to take the gloves to fill in for the game. In knowing anticipation that I probably wasn't going to get a bowl in the game, I was the first of two people to raise their hands; the other being Brett. So, instead of instigating a team domestic, Brett and I mutually decided that he would keep for the first 20 overs and myself the second half. I did think however, I had possibly drawn the short straw in our negotiations, as standing back to the stumps is typically easier than standing up; however, I didn't let this phase me.

The game started rather poorly; with I believe Macknade achieving 275 from their allotted 40. With Brett having recently completed his pre-agreed 20 overs behind the sticks; it was my time to shine! I suppose with the opposition already in a commanding position by drinks, the pressure to put in a good keeping performance was not entirely paramount. However, even with this lack of stress, what followed made the entire team express feelings of complete shock and awe! So, there I was, taking possession of the necessary keeping equipment from my outgoing team associate. Getting ready to reproduce that same awful performance I produced one year earlier; crouched behind the wickets for the first delivery after the mid-innings intermission, where the batsman immediately skipped four-foot down the pitch! He had a huge swipe across the line; missed it; and before I could even comprehend what was happening, the ball nestled into my gloves. I instantly panicked, forgot I had to take the bails off, subsequently drop the ball and remembered that removing bails was exactly what was required! The batsman was so far down, he carried on walking; not even looking as to whether I would successfully accomplish his execution! This consequently meant I had an infinite amount of time to carry out my assigned duties, but I got there! My nerves were somewhat calmed, and the constructive observations from Brett that my hands were 'in the right place' only helped build my fledging confidence.

Although this was only a little mishap, I got my first dismissal behind the stumps! With Mark continuing to bowl his floaty off-spin with a hint of swing hybrid, and myself continuing to station myself in the only place I had experience; I was comfortable! Then before I knew it, my hands were in the right place again to snag my second dismissal; a catch standing up this time! Where then! Lighting struck three times towards the end of the innings; a second stumping! I couldn't believe it, and to be honest neither could anyone else! It simply fathomed belief, nothing other than a miracle! It had appeared I was somewhat of a natural, and perhaps, I should have listened to Grandpa all those years earlier!

Well — that's what I initially thought, until it dawned on me! I had tried this specialised discipline the year before and I was terrible! How has it happened that I could be so inept previously, but extraordinarily proficient now? Something must have happened! It then became abundantly clear what had just occurred. It must have been Grandpa bequeathing his keeping talents to me! I'm not suggesting miracles happen; however, knowing full well that my grandpa who died only one month before these events, wanted me to keep when he was alive, he must have ceremoniously passed his wicketkeeping abilities upon me! As quite evidently he did not require them anymore due to his permanent residence of living six-foot under in the Thanet Cemetery!

I am fully aware that what you have just read must seem like a pile of nonsense. But it must be recognised, that one does not simply learn attributes and skills they have not practised and refined previously! This, in my opinion was only Grandpa's doing! I for one am very grateful, so much so, that I now keep wicket on a regular basis in the years since. This has not only allowed for many more happy memories playing cricket, but ultimately, would have made Grandpa proud that I also take great life fulfilment and satisfaction playing the game in such a similar nature to himself, that he so cherished for the duration of his life!

Grandpa Preparing to Open the Batting

Some of his Teammates

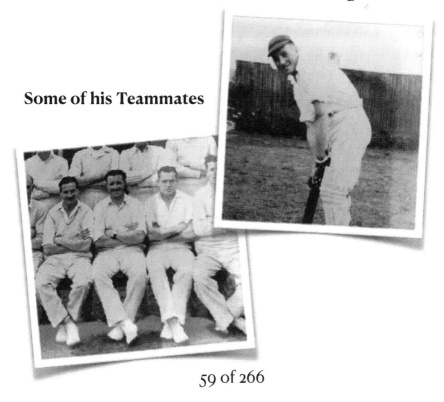

Scorecard from one of Grandpa's 100's

J. & E. HALL v. THOMAS & EDGE.

Played at New Eltham on Sunday, resulting in a win for Hall's. The feature of the game was a splendid innings of 117 not out by P. Clarke. Hall's young opening batsman, who for the second time this season carried his bat through the innings. Score:—

J. & E. HALL.

F. Gausden, lbw b Moore	33
P. Clarke, not out	117
A. Reynolds, lbw b Moore	9
E. Roberts, c Fishburn, b Tinker	5
J. Toon, b Tinker	29
O. Coker, b Tinker	1
W. Tibble, c Lovett, b Williams	29
S. Packer, b Tinker	5
R. Snow, b Burns	4
M. De Brie, c and b Tinker	15
J. Lincoln, not out	14
Extras	
(For 9 wkts. dec.)	256

THOMAS AND EDGE.

A. Fishburn, c Gausden b Tibble	19
B. Brico, c Reynolds b Toon	0
A. Tinker, b Toon	12
C. Burns, b Toon	2
S. Moore, lbw b Toon	18
A. Wiggins, c Tibble b Coker	58
E. Lovett, b Gausden	12
J. Williams, c Clarke b Coker	0
S. Hawn, c Gausden b Coker	0
D. Hardy, c Clarke, b Coker	0
Burns, not out	

I've got absolutely no idea what he's doing here!

TURNING 18: THE RUNS INCREASE AND SO DOES THE WEIGHT! - 2012

What a 12 months the year 2012 was! In a year where London held the summer Olympics; Her Majesty the Queen celebrated 60 years on the throne, and I scored over 700 runs at a whole season average of over 27! All whilst turning 18! Not only was it an eventful period in terms of national festivities and individual sporting accomplishments, I additionally surpassed one other personal milestone that I'm not as proud to disclose; my bodyweight nudged past 18 stone. As you read that previous declaration, I know what you must be thinking; but Josh, you were chubby in your youth and a sizeable teenager thereafter; no wonder you were the size of an elephant! I would be inclined to agree with that deduction; however, your rationale behind your inference could be clouded slightly.

Throughout my playing days at Margate, we, like all responsible alcohol selling licensees, had the rigorous rule that no one under the age of 18 was allowed to buy or drink alcoholic beverages on the ground. So, when I finally turned the legal age to supersede this stringent regulation, quite literally the flood gates opened! It must; however, be acknowledged, that all while the previous tales occurred, alcoholic beverages were a well-known quantity to my lifestyle at home; consistently imbibing in social gatherings and parties safely. However, when the figurative prohibition was lifted on the 15th May 2012, this 'imbibing' turned into a completely different beast. As such, when my 18th birthday fell more or less towards the start of the cricket season, I was able to exploit my newfound drinking freedoms to consistently enjoy social gatherings after most games.

With the amplified quantities of alcohol consumed in 2012, this inherently brought about issues typically associated with drinking. It was after one away Saturday league fixture vs Street End CC in July, where I had my usual two pints after the game. As such, these pints caused a, somewhat, significant neglect for the tour cap I had worn ever since we were first given them in 2006! This caused great mental distress, as how on earth could I play the Sunday fixture the following day without my treasured cap!?! Dad was able to utilise his practical initiative by seeking the Street End captain's contact details via the league booklet, to which the end result was that their skipper would post the hat. This was originally accepted by Dad, but clearly, I would not have my hat to play the Sunday game! So, after a temper tantrum and minor mental breakdown, off Dad and I went to the other side of Canterbury to fetch my precious 2006 Norfolk tour hat that Sunday morning. Fortunately, Dad was able to bend a few speeding laws and highway regulations to arrive in time to collect my hat whilst also making it in time for the game vs Deal Victoria CC. Not that the hat helped mind you; I didn't bowl, didn't keep, opened the batting and scored eight. So, yes, due to my inattentive memory, a morning was well spent!

This being said, the drinking malarkey clearly had a detrimental effect on my increased mass, as unsurprisingly, my diet was also terrible and calorie-dense. Mind you, although I was a big lad, this did come with some supplementary benefits; the sight of me strolling to the popping crease before the start of each innings drew a reaction of trepidation and terror in the minds of every opposition! As it happened, my large frame instilled the ability to strike a considerably long ball — along the floor; all whilst providing a stonewall defence to only infrequently give a whiff of taking my wicket!

On a side note, my social attitude from external 3rd parties because of my size appeared to also have other unintended positive consequences. In the August of that year, we as a club hired a coach for roughly fifty members to venture up to Lord's to watch the England ladies play Australia. My apparent influence with the ladies was clearly so infectious; it definitely looked like Sarah Taylor and Jenny Gunn simply couldn't keep their hands off me! I clearly jest — I'm surprised I even let them touch me! Which was probably good for me a no one wanted in their right mind would want to touch fat Josh in 2012!

The 2012 Lord's Trip with Sarah Taylor and Jenny Gunn

Oh How I Love this Hat!

The First Ton: The Start of the Annoying Batting Quirk - 2013

After the antics with forgetting my hat the previous summer, and the newfound freedom that a six-week summer holiday allowed for a practising teaching assistant; one Friday in late July we found ourselves playing a timed match against a touring side; Nuthurst CC. On what was probably the hottest day of the year in 2013, I foolishly decided that batting all afternoon in pursuit of my maiden hundred was a good idea! It was not. After Ian forfeited the toss, Nuthurst unwisely elected to field first. While donning the now seven-year-old tour cap, I was informed that I would be opening the batting with Ant Garcia. Needless to say, it was a slow start; accumulating 29 in our opening gambit, with myself the primary suspect to our leisurely beginning. I distinctly remember that due to the soaring heat and accompanying blinding light refracting off the one decent pitch annually produced at Tivoli Meadow, that my sight of the early deliveries was somewhat hindered. Even nicking-off early doors to a wicketkeeper clearly wielding teflon-lined gloves!

As lunchtime transitioned into mid-afternoon; I was able to see the opening bowlers off; the light became ever-so-slightly less offensive, and in the process finally middled one past mid-on for four. I felt 'set' and was ready for a 'biggen'. With three quick wickets falling in rapid succession, Brett subsequently arrived at the crease. We concluded that after a sensible start, it would be a failure to cricket if we did not stick around till the end. So, in true 'Josh' fashion, I was able to bring up my half century at a strike rate of a nudge over sixty, and along with it, the fifty partnership. What happened next has never happened in the years since, it was as if Bruce Banner had transformed into the Incredible Hulk! I don't remember much about the second half of this sweat perspiring innings, apart from the fact the ball started to travel to destinations I wasn't even aware I could send it to! One minute an immaculately timed backward cut was dismissed towards the point boundary, and the next, mission control (i.e. my bat) launched rockets destined for mars over long-on! I don't know what got into me, it was like everything just clicked and moulded together in sweet unison.

When I look back at that innings, it might have been due to what was the start of probably the most annoying quirk for any umpire or opposing player has even experienced; the endless checking and re-checking of my guard. It began in this innings and has continued to this day. Essentially, whenever I swap ends, for example running a single, I get the compelling urge to ask the umpire for my guard again once back on strike. This drilled behaviour even has to be requested at the start of a new over, even if I haven't swapped ends! The bat doesn't even have to be in the right place! All my ears need to hear is the umpire's gradually deteriorating monotone voice of;

"*Yes... that's middle...*"

For whatever reason, because I began this habit in the innings I made a ton, it has endured the test of time, and in turn, test every umpire's withering patience, as it is still practised today in 2019!

Anyway, I digress. After Bruce Banner scored his steady fifty and the Hulk now seizing the show; I soon found myself on 98 with one ball left before tea and our inevitable declaration. It was quite literally now or never! After being provided with the valuable information next to the scoreboard by the blatantly obviously adjacent numerals of nine and eight next to each other. It was for all to see! I knew I was on 98; Nuthurst knew I was on 98; and if I'm being honest, I think the whole of China knew I was on 98! Running to the other end and back was the only thing on my mind. All I needed was bat on ball and I was in with a fighting chance of ascending to the rank of 'Margate cricket club legend'! As the returning opening bowler ran in to deliver his final attempt to castle me; he produced probably the best ball he could; a yorker just shy of the intended length but on my stumps. After spending the previous 38.5 overs in the company of Nuthurst, the unrelenting heat, and half my team; I was seeing it quite literally like a beach ball! This was a delivery that could have quite easily bowled someone fresh to the crease; however, I was not fresh; I was sweaty; I was exhausted; but most importantly, I — was — ready! In the only shot that was easily accessible in my frail state, I middled a drive past Brett's feet at the other end, into a gap relatively straight. With the first of the necessary runs all but assured all I had to concern myself with was personally turning my 18 stone mass around 180 degrees and run up the other end to complete this myth like innings. I was safe in the knowledge that Brett wasn't doing anything other than running two, so all I had to do was worry about myself. As I slid my bat in to complete the first run and pushed off my right leg to commence the home straight; I suddenly got this merciless spasm in my left calf! It was like an IRA sniper had taken a leave of absence from his Northern Ireland posting, and ventured down to Margate for a jolly boys' outing to shoot a 45-calibre projectile in my leg from Tivoli Woods! This relentless cramp in my calf was not however going to stop me! So, as if I were Forest Gump running through the Vietnam war zone to save Bubba, or like Theresa May continuing her limping administration after her 3rd failed attempt of passing her faulty EU withdrawal agreement; I ran through my mortal injury!

As I neared the completion of the 100th run, I propelled my round, plump frame over the popping crease to realise this historically momentous achievement! Everyone went crazy! It must be said though, that due to this, I was unable to fully enjoy accomplishing the feat, primarily as I remained in that prone position for at least ten minutes! Ian was the first to rush on to congratulate me on my maiden hundred, and to stretch the perpetually spasming muscle. It felt like he had become permanently attached to my foot when the leg seizure decided to eventually submit! From memory, I think we lost the game, but that didn't matter as it was only a friendly! I had made it! I could finally say that I had scored a hundred! I could finally call myself a batsman!

Tale Epilogue

As an afterword, in bringing up my hundred, another ton came to pass that day. One between Brett Kirk and myself; Josh Williamson. The only reason I make note of this historic batting syndicate is simply because this feat has never been repeated in the years since! As I write these tales in the year 2019, this was the one and only day Brett and I have ever amassed a significant quantity of runs together. At the time of writing, we have shared the same cricket field virtually every game between April and September for 11 years, and only once have we built a batting partnership worth any merit, let alone a hundred. Needless to say, that because of this extraordinary statistic, there have been several run outs and numerous miscommunications in the middle! But that is not a story for now.

The Century Trophy Awarded at the 2013 End of Season Presentations

WESTGATE 6'S : BEER PONG AND THE SUBSEQUENT CONSEQUENCES - 2013

As it happens, 2013 was an action-packed year. After the metaphorical IRA sniper's jolly down to Margate, two weeks later in early August, we formed a team to contest in the 2nd, and currently last, annual Westgate 6's. Now, for anyone that isn't aware of what a 6's game comprises of; it's two teams of six in a five over hit; played on a full-size cricket field. I needn't make the obvious point that the primary objective of the tournament wasn't actually to play cricket, but more simply to act as the background entertainment while engaging in other drinking related activities. To give some considerable praise to the organisers at Westgate cricket club, the day was thoughtfully constructed by only scheduling four games, plus a final for each participating team; even innocently provided us with extra amenities such as beer pong and cheap drinks to carry us through the lull periods of the long day.

The day started so well; winning the first two games with relative ease. This; however, is where our achievements in the cricket made a remarkable halt, and our success in drinking shenanigans commenced! So, the clock struck noon, and the consumption of intoxicating beverages began! This is where the opening ceremony for the beer pong had formally taken place. It goes   without saying that as a team we had all telepathically designated that winning a beer pong tournament was far more important, and hence replaced the original objective of succeeding in the cricket 6's! Clearly, our main reason for being there that day had now appeared to have become a subsidiary partner to the proceedings moving forward.

In conjunction with Ant, where both of us were a bit of a demon at darts and weighing in at a hefty amount, all bets were suspended on one of our inevitable victories. This being a knockout affair, I sailed past JP who he himself fell foul to my pin-point accuracy! Needless to say, this theme continued until the final where I met my nefarious foe. Fortunately for me, we conveniently heard the loud bellow to play in our final group game of the day. This call couldn't have come soon enough as the alcohol was now taking a strong hold over my most basic coordination skills, resulting in a boost of confidence to my cricket abilities. If I'm being honest, it was much akin to the King of Sparta, nothing could stop me!

The last game was Margate vs Nelson, always a fiery contest, and this would be no different! With us fielding first, and myself not required to don the keeping gloves on this occasion; Brett set the field, where he utilised my erratic fielding skills at long-off. Nelson got off to a reasonable start, realising 20 runs from the first two overs. With myself standing there, quite clearly half-cut and not a clue of what was going on around me; the 'in' batsman sent a well-struck, fairly 'flattish', drive in the air my way. Now, for anyone who's witnessed my fielding prowess, knows full well it's a bit like a box of chocolates; you don't know what you're going to get. So, when this ball came hurtling towards the general vicinity of my chubby face, I was left with two options; either catch the ball or move out the way and let it go for six. Clearly, option two was not a viable alternative as this would have let the team down; the club down; but most importantly, let my spartan like drunk persona down. As I didn't have to move, I simply had to catch it, dropping it would have also drawn unfavourable consequences. Having finished four games of beer pong previously, it was literally a 50/50 chance, as by this point, I was seeing double! Do I position my hands on the left ball or right? In the end, I did neither; so just like a petrified child, both my hands were held up over my face in the middle of both options. Unsure of the accuracy of my decision, as the fast approaching cricket ball neared my palms', I didn't know whether I was going to get a fistful of leather or a mouthful! Luckily for me, a fistful was exactly how the dust settled on this little predicament; the batsman was off the field, and in three overs I would be too!

Chasing 40 off five overs, this was a fairly easy target to reach in this form of the game. So, in true skipper fashion, Brett led the troops into battle and opened. I can't remember whether we won or lost this game, but that doesn't matter, what did happen could have easily made it on to ITV's 'You've been framed'! With Nelson utilising an all too common tactic in limited over games, they elected to open their innings with a loopy off-spinner. I mean, this guy was awful, Brett could have quite easily seen most of the target off in the first six deliveries. This; however, did not happen. I will give Brett some credit though, he struck a well-timed drive for four and agriculturally mooed one over cow for six, so he did get us a quarter of the way there; however, when he attempted to push the next ball in the gap at cover for a scampered two, this loopy off break bowler managed to produce the most vicious pop off a length that only the world's best couldn't even organically achieve! Brett clearly didn't foresee this impending circumstance and continued his ill-fated endeavours of pushing the gap for two. To which he copped the sharp rising ball to his face! This caused an ever-so delectable gash on his above averagely sized money maker, and promptly rushed himself off to the nearest accident and emergency! Although initially concerned for his immediate welfare, once it was established that he wasn't going to die, this caused great collective amusement that this slow, loopy bowler had caused an injury sufficient to warrant a trip to the hospital!

Moving swiftly back to this tale's priority. Once Brett was safely on his way to occupy a health practitioner's time, the moment for the real final of the day was ready to commence; the final of the Margate ad-hoc inter-club beer pong knockout cup! After my initial saviour in the form of a cricket intermission, I could no longer hide from my evident inebriation. After trudging my way through a closely fought semi final, I was pitted against the joint-favourite, Ant. To save you from the finer intricacies of my opponent, at the time, Antonio was considerably older than myself, half a foot taller and five stone heavier; I knew a battle was on my hands! As was customary in our pre-agreed competition regulations, the opposing player chose your drink. So, Ant being Ant, he was made privy to the rather pertinent detail that I'm somewhat 'averse' to consuming Fosters; most notably because I think it has an aftertaste that's reminiscent of stale rat urine! However, I knew Guinness was his kryptonite! The contest had a certain 'ebb and flow' feeling to it, with both slowly whittling each others' cups down; Ant more efficiently than myself though. With three needed to win against Ant's one, I missed my shot and hence surrendered possession of the ping-pong ball. If he sunk this next shot, not only would have I have to finish my Foster's, but three of his Guinness'! So, in what appeared to be slow motion, Ant drew back his right elbow and flung the ball out of his impeccably cocked wrist. You could have mistaken this event for something out of a Hollywood blockbuster film; in what felt like multiple seconds; not moments; the ball slowly arched dangerously close towards my last cup. It hit the inside lip and started to swirl around the rim! Together with a huge sigh expelled from the crowd's mouth, no one quite knew which way it was going to go. With the ball continuing to perpetually circle the rim of my last cup; it went around and around and around and around, and suddenly! The 'plonk' of death. The ball intimately floated on top of the heavy froth. I had lost. As penance, I had to finish mine and Ant's beer. My Fosters wasn't too bad as I already had eight glasses in the lead up; it was my favourite drink of choice that had me in trouble! The first Guinness went down fairly smoothly. The second; I got a slight stomach rumbling, but as I got two-thirds into downing the third and final tribute; the recent digestive concerns instantaneously morphed into a re-appearing magic act! Not only did I reacquaint myself with the first and second Guinness, but after a timely retreat to the ladies toilet, I had sight of my prior victories, as well as the multiple burgers and hotdogs from the BBQ! It went everywhere! Worst of all, I attempted to clear it up to show remorse for what I had just done, but due to my domestic ineptness, the lady behind the bar had to finish! Ant, who had already caused enough torment and embarrassment for the day, thought it would also be a good idea to call my mother and inform her of my day's multi-textured produce! She arrived in what felt like minutes, and consequently marched me swiftly home for an early shower!

All things considered, to this day, I still don't know who won the cricket tournament!

The End Result of the Beer Pong Tournament

THE WORKS LEAGUE CUP WIN - 2014

The 2014 season, an interesting year. I strung together a number of respectable performances with the bat, while also led the club to its 5th straight works league cup win! The works league was a Thanet based competition that was originally designed to facilitate amateur cricket to workers on a midweek evening. In the league's hay day, they had three, maybe even four divisions, all striving to be the best in a FA cup style knockout tournament! These good times are sadly gone for the league and in the years since has unfortunately disbanded; however, in 2014 there was a fairly strong appetite for this variety of the game which created a few bitter rivalries! As it happened, one could probably view the cup competition as a little like the FA community shield; the same two teams competing in the same final, year after year after year. This was the year Margate, a team who played roughly seven divisions lower than their opposition in terms of Saturday Kent league cricket, stood in the face of adversity to beat the overwhelming odds against them to beat the giants of Thanet cricket; Broadstairs.

As was now customary; Margate and Broadstairs rotated the venue for the final every year. It was the turn of Broadstairs to host this year's showcase. In a break from the typical rules of the works league, the final was always 20 overs a side as opposed to the regular 16. With myself skippering the side; the pitch could have been a soft, luminous green track and I still would have batted first. So, after winning the toss and using my now well-developed cricket brain, due to an understandable lack of floodlights at this level of the game, batting was always the preferred option. Opening up with the now consistent pairing of Jamie and Sam they got us off to a flyer! Scoring 52 for the 1st wicket partnership. This theme continued for the duration of the innings, with only Neil and Brett in the top eight not achieving double figures. In contempt for my own fast scoring batting skills, I elected to bat at eight to ensure we got off to a good started without any unnecessary stalls. This was an effective tactic, which must be said that due to my now even larger frame from the ton last summer, this ploy naturally forced me into a significant amount of running between the wickets! Not letting this deter me, I started slowly in this useful tail-end innings; nudging a few around to get myself into the swing of it. After dragging myself to five not out, and the team on an already defendable total, I eyed up the bowling of this young leg spin bowler who I believe is now well rooted within the Kent academy structure. Yes, I can hear you all thinking;

"But Josh, that's bullying, pick on someone your own size".
This, however, was not the time for mercy; it was the time to dominate and send Broadstairs packing! After giving his first ball a look, I put him into a false sense of security and intentionally 'agriculturally mooed' inside a delivery outside my

off peg. Again, this was a good tactic as it was designed to exploit the young bowler's naivety in playing adult cricket and trick him into repeating his original dosage. He did just that! The ball floated up above my eye line; dropped down on to the pitch in line with my 4th stump, and then — it sailed up and up and up and up, until it was in the fielder's hands at long-on! I wasn't out however, in the process of 'mitting' the rocket, he fell over the white boundary marker directly in front of the engrossed spectating crowd! Six runs!

Although the reward was sweet! The means to achieve it, unfortunately, was not. This close call was enough for this 18 stone lump to result in a return to the 'running game'. I continued for another over until it became abundantly obvious for all to see, that it was now a case of getting out, hitting out, or calling 999. Being a stubborn and obstinate mule, that treats their wicket like their very own life; getting out on purpose was not an option. Whereas, by this stage of proceedings, 'hitting out' was no longer a viable alternative either, due to the grossly insufficient supply of available oxygen, and omitting a beautiful 'whitish' glow; not wholly dissimilar to that of Casper the Friendly Ghost! It was clearly the '999' option or get out trying! So, in true belligerent fashion, I calculatedly pushed the next ball to midwicket with just enough power to provide time for a quickly scampered two. Well — this was the plan anyway. After successfully negotiating part one and two of executing the idea and sprinting the initial run; part three was my inevitable downfall! As I turned my round body around to initiate the second run, the fielder already had the ball in his hands, I knew this wasn't going to end well! So, to provide you with an analogy for this fruitless endeavour would be to describe my struggle in the words of the German philosopher; Friedrich Nietzsche;

> *"One should die proudly when it is no longer possible to live proudly".*

These words certainly described my supporting innings that day, and so, much like a lame horse, it was best to put the figurative shotgun to my short but sweet innings.

So, there I was, staggering back to the pavilion, wondering whether I was going to be joining Grandpa in the Heavens, when the outline of this guardian angel's silhouette focused into blurred view. It was my mother! Rushing to my aid, she presented me with this most succulent ice lolly and a pint of water! I was saved! Within minutes I had caught my breath back, I could walk, my skin's pinkness was returning, and I was back to full fitness, ready to occupy my self-imposed position of wicketkeeping half a foot behind the bowling crease.

With Margate attainting a lofty 184 in our allotted 20 overs, it was a big ask for the Kent League Division Two club. It didn't start well for them, losing their first wicket in the opening over after a precisely thrown attempt from Dan Carter into my gloves for a timely runout. Broadstairs were never really in the run chase, only amassing 110 in their futile reply. We walked off winners and five-time champions of this historic cup! Margate in practice, a team seven leagues below their opposition outshone Broadstairs in their own backyard, and with it, local cup glory! The award ceremony was sweet, with home onlookers conceding that their precious town club were thoroughly outplayed in every discipline; batting, bowling, fielding, and apparently, even running between the wickets by a robust opposing captain.!We fully enjoyed every moment! Perhaps, myself more than most! So, in a similar vein to Bruce Bogtrotter, after he devoured that huge chocolate cake in Matilda, I had the customary honours of holding aloft the large silver cup that only 46 other captains had held before me! I could finally celebrate not only my team's victory, but also my own competition win as a captain!

Pictures Celebrating the Win!

The 2014 Works League Cup Winning Team

THE GREAT WEIGHT-LOSS BET - 2014

Up until this point in the chronology of memoirs, there has been a running theme of self-indulgence (both figuratively and literally) in terms of casting jokes about my problems with childhood obesity. On the 4th of August 2014, at the age of twenty years, two months and twenty days; I began a journey, which at the time felt like the first steps of climbing Mount Everest; to lose the weight I so ceremonially gained from the day I was born! The seed of motivation for such an enormous cause began life two weeks prior at an away game to Littlebourne. In consultation with Ant Garcia, the same man who was accountable for the beer pong chunder; we decided that as we both needed to shed some excess body weight from our well-built frames, and that to engage in a friendly wager would be of benefit to our on-going health. It was agreed that as cricket week directly followed the result of this light-hearted exchange, that to commence proceedings immediately would not have been the best of starts!

So, there we were every day during cricket week, enjoying what was effectively a seven day 'last supper', to gain every possible incentive to take this bet seriously. From memory, I consumed copious amounts of beer, bacon burgers and buffets every evening from a variety of stereotypical international cuisines. I had a great time! One evening it was pasta and beer, another is was chilli — and beer. Nothing was going to stop me in the lead up to the inventible arrival of Monday the 4th of August, 2014. Full of inspiration that I now possessed the necessary extrinsic motivation via the bet, and the crucial intrinsic impetus due to the massive food feast the week prior, I was now ready to start the ascent! Or 'decent' as the case may be!

After conducting some essential research surrounding other peoples' endeavours to lose weight; I concluded that two things were indispensable to a possible success story; an application called 'MyFitnessPal' which allowed users to keep close track of their daily nutrition, and; to schedule time to participate in low-impact exercise. Without hesitation, the app was downloaded, where I was also able to procure an un-loved rowing machine to greet me every morning to meet the exercise objective. Due to my compulsive mindset and regimented routines because of my ASD; using the calorie counter app was great! Every time I ate something, it went into the app! Nothing could have been easier! The rowing machine; however, didn't last too long. After two workouts, and endless sore knees for days, I gave up on that idea. In principle, it was fool proof! In practice, not so much. This lacking exercise factor didn't matter though, within two weeks I had lost 14 pounds and was a touch over 17 stone. So, as the end of the cricket season turned into autumn, the autumn into winter, my motivation did not perish along with the year 2014; it only grew as my waistline shrunk!

Before I knew it, it was the 2015 cricket season and I was 15 stone! I had lost three stone in the winter months, which one could say was simply influenced by my ASD ritualistic brain into continuing my accomplishments. At this point, no additional exercise apart from indoor cricket was required, where apparently because of a sufficiently high enough energy deficit I lost weight; it seemed my own body consuming its own fat stores was enough!

As the months progressed, it appeared that I no longer required the external stimulus of the wager with my large teammate, losing weight for myself and for my own health benefit was sufficient to elaborate upon the initial 42-pound loss over the winter of 2014. Good job really, as it emerged at the start of the 2015 season that Ant, due to some personal issues, had actually put on weight over the winter. My well-formed and rounded conscience would not allow myself to claim the previously agreed financial remuneration from the victory, so in replacement of any monetary gain, I accepted that the real prize was me. I felt better about myself, had limitless confidence and suddenly I was obtaining looks from strangers of the opposite sex! But that's a string of stories for the next chapter!

Evidently, life was good. I put myself in a situation where my body didn't stand out when starting University in the

September of 2015, and as such, the reason for my existence on this planet was beginning to fall into place. For the interest of time in this somewhat long-winded tale and fast-forwarding to 2016. I weighed ten and a half stone because of my new-found enjoyment of running during the first of three University summers'. This was all well and good but unfortunately, I began to look like a white Ethiopian marathon runner, and possibly even began showing the signs of an eating disorder! I was so fixated to never put weight on again! However, I came to realise this issue, and promptly drew back on the amount of running and the severity of my self-imposed nutrition austerity measure, to find the right balance.

It must be said that I have never stopped counting calories even to this day in 2019 as I have continued my close totalitarian food regime ever since! I still have the stomach of a fat man when I put my mind to it though. However, it is at this point before we continue into the years of 2015 and beyond, that because of that decision in August of 2014, it quite possibly provided me with the chances and opportunities to help me become the man I am today!

GALLERY OF THE WEIGHT LOSS 2014 - 2019

14/8/14

**Day One Of The New
Lifestyle in 2014**

8/8/19

**Day *'God Knows What'* Of The New
Lifestyle in 2019**

21/8/15

9/5/16

15/5/15

29/6/17

10/7/18

CHAPTER FOUR:

LIFE IN THE 20'S (THE BILLY YEARS) : 2015 - 2019

CHAPTER PROLOGUE

As this series of short stories transitions into the somewhat recent past. This final chapter will, in essence, continue the same theme of cricket but reminisce upon events that aren't directly related to 'in-game' events. As such, for mainly comedic purposes, I will be drawing upon memories that include my best friends and teammates that I have built throughout my playing days.

WHEN BRETT AND JOSH MET BILL - 2015

This memoir plans to flesh out one of the more, shall I say, 'prominent characters' for the remainder of this series of life memoirs. Good Friday of 2015 was the day that myself and Brett, whom I have known for many years, met William Charles Woollard. Or more colloquially known as Billy. Now, Billy is an 'interesting' soul, and to set the scene for that now notorious day, it was cold and 'damp' to say the least. We were netting that bank holiday for one sole purpose; to see if Billy was any good. Before his arrival, he had 'bigged' up his previous playing history with our then club captain, Ian Robinson; stating he had played in the lofty heights of the Kent League and was a useful all rounder.

So, myself, Brett, Ian, Harry Carter and one other whom I can't remember were there having already started this net well before Billy's arrival. We were freezing cold and beginning to wonder whether the only reason we were there in the first place would even turn up! Some time had elapsed and all of us were getting a little worried, where when I believe Harry was nearing the end of his time batting; we saw this somewhat distinguishably round figure appear from the other side of the ground! So, in something similar to the film 'The Shining', when Jack Nicholson abruptly broke through the toilet door. We suddenly noticed this 'well-set' gentleman emerge from the gap in the hedge and stagger across the width of the dew-laden Tivoli Meadow field. Looking back, knowing what I know now in 2019; instead of the quote "*Heeeere's Johnny*"; substituting the name 'Johnny' for 'Billy' would absolutely not be out of place!

Billy greeted the group and obviously expanded upon his previous track record with the rest of us, where he promptly picked up this excessively damp cricket ball; marked out this run-up; and proceeded to, what looked like from my perspective, try his unequivocal hardest to make a good first impression with the club he now ultimately calls home years later. With me, Brett and Ian all watching with great anticipation to establish whether we had wasted our time netting in this dismal weather; Bill ran in with what I perceived as some serious intent and fired down what must have been a 70mph out swinger! We all instantly looked at each other, didn't utter a word and gave this approving nod that yes, this was time well spent; Billy was decent! We didn't say anything until after the session, but this was primarily to not give the game away of what we thought of this new player and continued our practice in the knowledge that we had probably signed a new player for the forthcoming season! Well — I mean, in 2015 I was actually the top run scorer in all cricket, but nevertheless, he was a nice addition.

Little did we know at the time, if another week had elapsed following the initial net session, Billy has since enlightened us that he would have joined Corinthians CC instead, and if I'm being honest, the remainder of this book would be a little dull!

So, enjoy this forthcoming chapter; it's a hell of a ride!

A Series of Short Cricket Week Tales : 2015 - 2017

This next section will incorporate the most pertinent stories with the underlying premise of Margate cricket club's annual cricket week. The years in which these occurred will be in no particular sequential order. Primarily because for the interest of effectively structuring the book (and the fact I can't actually remember what years they occurred!), this is simply the best way of writing this section.

1) The Nearly Fatal Campfires

As was now a well-rehearsed tradition at Tivoli Meadow; cricket week is where all the loyal patrons of the seven-day event, pitched up tents next to the nets on the far side of the ground, to enjoy nightly campfires under the stars. Why we endured this long-practised ritual? I will never know, as every time the fire was lit, there was never any intention of sleeping! I remember it was one year, when there were a good number of cricket week regulars who elected to continue the festivities after the bingo evening to start the campfire, where it soon became perfectly apparent that none of us possessed the requisite 'scouting' attributes to start said fire! There were several cigarette lighters floating about in peoples' pockets, but nothing adequately sufficient to instigate a five-foot high blaze.

Upon a 'well thought out' proposal from Bill, he suggested that we utilised some unleaded petrol to get the after-party going! So, there we both were, in the groundsman's shed searching for fuel under torchlight, where it goes without saying, we were successful in our quest! After playing the role of the willing accomplice in obtaining the flammable liquid; the part of the 'twisted fire starter' in this hazardous production was promptly assumed by Bill. Without thinking through this process particularly well, he doused the stacked pile of wood with the petrol, and instead of simply throwing his lighter into the pre-prepared death trap, he elected to light the end of a somewhat short stick and gradually move it towards the doused wood. I mean this 'twig' could have only been about a foot! So, with Billy standing mere inches from an excruciating roasted demise, he steadily moved his right hand towards the un-lit campfire; WHOOF! Billy was now solely in the hands of the cricket campfire gods as the blaze instantaneously graduated ten foot into the air and with it, his face considerably flushed and possibly scorched in the process! We could have quite easily seen a rendition of the 'stop, drop and roll' manoeuvre, while also featuring in the next episode of NCSI providing eye witness accounts to the local constabulary as to why our friend was reduced to a caracoled cadaver! If that worst-case scenario had come to pass, we wouldn't have even been able to assist our cooking mate! The only source of water we had in a close enough vicinity would have been mixed with hops and barley, and thus, quite literally would have only added fuel to the ten-foot-high fire!

Fortunately, for him and for us, the cricket week deities looked favourably upon a blessed William Woollard that fateful night. He didn't cook to a cinder and is still happily alive in 2019! Having said that, this in itself is a bloody miracle, as he repeated this whole death-defying act two days later when invariably another campfire was irresponsibly created for the communal benefit of our time-honoured tradition, with again, you guessed it, petrol

Before

After

2) THE CONSECUTIVE SHAGGINGS'

Before I get delve particularly deep into this 'short but sweet' tale. I will make it perfectly clear that this memoir positions myself as an observant 3rd party, and hence not the active participant. It was Tuesday of the 2016 cricket week when, again, my good friend Billy completed his season's long conquest of occupying some 'friendly' time with one of the player's daughters. I have elected to not name names on this occasion as it was felt that this story would not be universally welcomed by all potential memoir personalities.

Anyway, after an already eventful evening with the bingo and Bill's previous death-defying exploits. A group of six cricket week faithfuls; all tired and drunk, formed the well-rehearsed semi-circle around the blazing campfire. As it happened, four of us were positioned on one side, and in what could have been only a premeditated enterprise from William, was himself and his consensual prey the other. After an hour or so of some timeless musical classics, such as, 'Hotel California' by the Eagles and 'Bohemian Rhapsody' by Queen; a couple of the campfire enthusiasts decided to call time on this midweek folly and called it a night (or morning as was the case). With myself at this point acutely oblivious as

Billy Making His Move!

to the current external endeavours, and Brett, who evidently was conscious; Billy and his un-named mark edged closer and closer as each song reached its inevitable conclusion. There was me singing to the top of my lungs with Brett and Billy accompanying me, while Billy was also 'inconspicuously' ushering his left hand higher and higher up his female friend's thick-set thighs under the concealing blanket.

Uh oh!

Clearly, after a short period of time imbibing in this promiscuous activity; Billy grew tired of the public illustration of ineffective foreplay and proceeded to whisper in the ear of his eventual conquest. I don't know what was communicated, but it must have been effective! Billy and his newfound playmate made their way to his tent. This was not before Brett quietly conveyed what was actually happening to me, where we agreed to make our own way to our tents but set a timely rendezvous of five minutes next to the dying embers of the fire. The elapsed time felt like it was a long intermission; inspecting my phone every minute on the minute. With the time now passed, Brett and I simultaneously vacated our tents where we were immediately alerted to a defined sound of 'rustling' in the direction of the jointly occupied camp. It is at this point that I'll allow you to make your own deductions as to what was actually happening, but Brett and I both judged that it could have only of been one thing!

After silently making our way to scrutinise the accuracy of Brett's previous assumptions; you guessed it, it turned out he was absolutely right! With not a moment to spare, I peeked my recording phone into the tent's air vent and began filming the couple where I filmed Billy on top of his female mate! In the video, all one could see was the surname 'Woollard'. This was all until seconds passed when we heard the feminine voice utter the phrase *"Who the fuck is that?!?!"* Without hesitating for thought, Brett and I explode into great laughter; run away, and in the process; ruin Billy's and his consensual participant's early morning excursions!

With Bill's Tuesday attempts now spoiled, it wasn't even 48 hours until his next endeavour! Again, in what could have seemed like the beginnings of a regular foursome routine; Brett, me, Billy and the unnamed female were again occupied by the familiar indulgence of a blazing summertime campfire. In similar fashion to the Tuesday; music was blearing; the drink was flowing, and clearly, so was Billy's masculine appendage! In what could have only been a sign of goodwill from me and Brett; we ventured off to have a timely wee in the bushes and view the stars out of the light polluting campfire. This gave Billy, and his soon to be one-time lover adequate time to, how can I phrase it, 're-acclimatise' with each other. Not thinking they would actually do anything given the events of 2 days earlier; we concluded that sitting on the Astro pitch for 15 minutes should be an adequate amount of time to let fate take its course. So, off we went with a bottle of fizz and enjoyed the clear night's sky; discussing cricket, the stars and taking bets as to what we would find on our eventual return to the campfire circle. It was a peaceful inebriated portion of that evening, which only became increasingly humorous as time went on. What happened next accelerated at a rapid pace! I can't say I actually saw anything, but I have it on reliable account from Brett, that even from the middle of the square, all one could see was Billy, 'out the back' of his female accomplice on the boot of his newly bought second-hand Land Rover! Brett being the friend he is, elected to not intervene in this impending 2016 season eventuality, and allowed Bill to enjoy some 'short-lived' success. We eventually made our way back to the campfire, brought up the topic of the 'Land Rover' escapades, to which we got a pageant of laughter from Bill, and an expedited retirement to the outside sleeping arrangements from his newly acquainted companion!

Needless to say, we haven't let Billy's little regrettable excursion die!

A rather ominous looking 'W' and 'O'

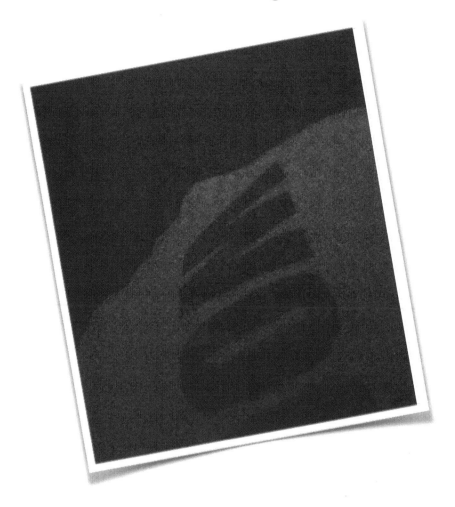

3) I Can See the Nets!

As I continue to write these cricket week campfire chronicles, it would be surely amiss of me to not document the first sight of 'netting' at the crack of dawn. I can hear the yawn creeping out your tightly closed mouth as you read that first sentence; however, as I go through my life, to allow the creation of this synonym for an 'all-nighter' to fall to the depths of history, would do not just myself, but all people present that night a serious disservice. The initial existence of 'seeing the nets' was actually after the already eventful week of the 2016 edition of cricket week. After several alcohol-fuelled nights of no sleep I became somewhat delusional; where the sun soon began to rise over Tivoli Meadow. Having positioned ourselves near the nets; one could not see anything at night, let alone the cricket practice facilities, due to the woven black thread being positioned in front of the pitch-black surroundings! So, when the early signs of dawn began to unveil itself upon us, one could immediately gain sight of the once invisible entwined structure! I consequently said, and I quote, *"I can see the nets!"* Everyone turned around and were utterly amazed at this revelation!

So, with myself not being mentally wired like other human beings, this somewhat obscure terminology became perfectly obvious for all my intoxicated peers. Hence, whenever there has been an 'all-nighter' in the years since, even if it is not held at the cricket club, when the phrase "I can see the nets" is utilised, without thought, it is recognised by all present to signify that the sun has indeed risen.

4) THE DEPRECATION OF TENTS

Although not keeping to the structure of the book, it must have been one of my first outings camping at our cricket week in 2012. Having just turned 18 and taking every opportunity to enjoy the delights of consuming copious amounts of alcohol, I withdrew from the parental shackles of my mother and father where I informed them that I would be staying at the club and consequently would not be coming home after the official evening entertainment. Mother wasn't too pleased but I did just that! Dad went into the shed, found his tent and gave me the strictest of instructions that I must look after it otherwise he would be most displeased!

The initial sequence of these events are, to be honest, a little hazy; however, it unfolded a little like this. From memory, it was, again, the time-honoured tradition of the bingo evening; Chris Carter was calling the numbers; adding in the well-known quips here and there as he saw fit;

"Six and nine, 69!" *cue inevitable cheering*.
"Two fat ladies, 88!"

"Legs eleven, 11" *cue wolf whistle*.

For whatever reason on this evening, I opted to drink Stella, otherwise universally known in British culture as; 'wife-beater'. Why? I really do not know; however, not knowing my tolerances to that particular beer, it apparently got a little out of hand when it came to the campfire! Anyway, the evening finished but the night had not begun!

In the now recognised standard entertainment of a collective campfire, the music went on for a little too long, where one could probably recollect what we now would call 'seeing the nets'. As such, everyone retired to their tents for some well-needed rest; however, not everyone actually did. With myself camping for the first time and far too drunk, in what appeared to be some MCC Satanist cult, this was the evening everyone else decided to initiate Josh into the cricket week rituals. With myself now fast asleep, not a creature was stirring, not even a mouse, apart from mice called Brett, James and Jamie! They undertook this ritual masked by undertones of my disruptive sleep pattern and the resulting deafening talking in my sleep; guy ropes were undone; urine was doused, and with it, the internal tent compartments were broken beyond repair as a result!

With the morning sun now blanketing my damp and broken outdoor sleeping arrangements. It was wasn't long before my father arrived to collect a tired teenager to resume his sleep in the comfort of his bed at home. Little did I know what happened the previous night while I was asleep! I was awoken to the resounding cries of anger that Dad's beloved tent was well and truly fucked! I will never forget the proceeding statements from Father ringing in my ear;

"Josh what have you done! You don't mess with tentage!"

I innately pointed the finger of blame towards Jamie; where Dad consequently stormed directly over to his tent, pulled him out via his left ear and showed him the drunk damage he imposed on Dad's poor tent. Jamie had no words, I had no words, so he threw the tent in the car and marched me back home to barracks! No words were spoken on that trip home...

I haven't told Dad this yet, but in the years since, when I look back, it probably was only the pee-soaked exterior and the removal of guy ropes that were attributable to Jamie et al,. Being the 18 stone heavy I was in those days, due to the inebriated state and a very high centre of gravity; I actually think I torpedoed myself into the tent while destroying the internal partition in the process! The addition of lukewarm humanistic waste was merely the cherry on top of this deconstructed cake! Sorry Dad!

5) THE GRAND PROJECTILE VOMITING

To conclude this lengthy section of cricket week tales, we end on a delightfully short note. To provide the year or even day in the week this tale happened currently escapes my memory, I think it might have been 2015, but I really do not know. But after one too many heavy and sleepless campfire mornings, ahem! I mean nights. My good friend Dan thought it'll be wise to follow through on his commitment to play the whole-day game on the Thursday, starting at 1pm. Needless to say, we lost the toss and were inserted to field in furnace like conditions. This only allowed this sorry predicament to unravel more expediently than it might have done so organically! Being the emerging pace bowler Dan was, the captain on the day, Brett, also provided him with the prestigious honours of opening the bowling in 30°C heat!

With myself in my now well-acquainted position of behind the sticks, I had a full view of the events that followed. Dan quite literally limped through the 1st over, then trudged off to fine leg for six balls and crawled through his second. But in the run up to the first delivery of his third, and might I also add, last over, he came to an emphatic halt at the popping crease. He bent over, put both of his hands on his knees, abruptly covered his mouth and ran over to the outfield bush to deposit the remains of the previous night's dinner! I saw what came out his mouth and one could only describe it luminous coloured vomit! The reason I draw upon this event, is because this shrubbery positioned in the middle of the outfield is actually an off-spur of the lime tree which was once the signature showcase of the St. Lawrence ground in Canterbury for over 100 years! Oh, how the mighty have fallen!

Nevertheless, to bring this story to a head. This self-inflicted state of the contents of Dan's stomach reappearing continued for what must have been a good five minutes! The umpire even had to stop the game, walk over to struggling 18-year-old and mutually agreed with him that the best course of action was to undertake a hastily retreat back to the clubhouse toilets and lie down for an unspecified amount of time. And Dan did just that, and from my fairly accurate recollection, didn't actually return to the game!

THE Eurovision Night - 2015

Bringing this monologue of cricketing tales back to the easily understandable chronological structure, we return with a story situated a week after my 21st birthday in the year 2015. I do not dare bring up the events of my score plus one celebration, as a certain personality for the remainder of this book wasn't invited due to his, then, recent undertaking of joining the club! However, I move swiftly on.

For those that may not be aware, that now not so much, but when growing up, the Williamsons' enjoyed the collective viewing of the Eurovision Song Contest every year without fail. Seeing that we had a strong and active membership in 2015, I instigated the decision to host a Eurovision party at the club after the Saturday league game. The events of this little soirée begun so well, with the majority of members remembering a pair of earplugs to block out the ear-piercing rubbish that Europeans' class the height of musical talent! The drinks were flowing, I was the only one enjoying the UK entry amongst others, while everyone universally took great pride in our country's inevitable end result of *"Nil poi"*. Evidently, I had, again, too much to drink and unavoidably had to make frequent visitations to the toilets to rectify the overconsumption of inebriating liquids. Now, for those that do not know, people with ASD often exhibit signs of needing a strict routine while also requiring firm regular positions in a familiar location. At the club, my firm regular position was located on the right hand seat of a two-person sofa with its back against the wall facing the television. Everyone knew this was my seat. Therefore, when I clearly need the occupation of said chair, and if a 3rd party were to lower one's self into the right hand cushion on the two-person sofa with its back against the wall facing the television, this would only cause a negative response for any enthusiastic provoker!

It was my fourth time of completing the visit to the little boys' room, where on re-admittance into the clubhouse lounge area, in an event that can only be compared to the start of World War One, after the shooting of Archduke Franz Ferdinand, I found said 'enthusiastic provoker' in the form of a certain Brett William Scott Kirk! I politely requested for his expedited departure from my emotionally reserved seat; no reaction. I asked him again; same result. Nothing other than physical intervention would suffice! I proceeded to sit on the legs of my newfound 'seat squatter' and attempted to push him off; again nothing! So, like in the desperate words of Ian Beal from EastEnders; *"I had nothing left!"* The only way to resolve this calamitous circumstance was to vacate the warmth of the MCC clubhouse, take my two-thirds-full pint of Guinness, and make haste in a humongous huff to the newly erected scorer's hut!

So, off I trudged to the green outhouse, where I must say, while sitting in that rickety wooden structure, just like some lost puppy, I naïvely thought,

> "Yeah! this will show them, they are bound to come and retrieve me any minute now, I will win this untimely, Eurovision missing protest, and never have to worry about their baiting behaviour again!"

This — did not happen. I savoured my newly poured pint for must have been a good half an hour, before I came to the stark realisation of my dire misjudgement! My friends were nowhere to be found anywhere near the vicinity of the score hut, let alone thinking about moving from their stolen seats. They were quite clearly cosied up in the warmth of the clubhouse while I was sat there like some utter retard, envisaging a favourable outcome. I clearly had no other option than to accept a humiliating defeat and beg for my seat back. They could see I was obviously distressed by this point, so eventually they did concede; however, I lost the war and consequently have had to fight in a fair few more battles.

Because this was such a big issue for me, they all thought I had been crying over their perceived figurative spilt milk, I had not. I was a big boy, admittedly I was angry, but I wanted revenge on Brett. Four years later this revenge did emerge, and Brett, did have his comeuppance, but that is a story for later.

Two Hours Until the Start: The Birth of Dylan! - 2015

This next story falls on Saturday the 25th of July, 2015. On a day where the first team had their game conceded to them; we were subsequently greeted to a few 'guest appearances' representing the Margate topflight in the second team fixture at home. You guessed it from the title; on a day where his son was born, one of those 'guest appearances' was none other than Billy Woollard.

To provide you with some useful context as to the background situation around the said birth of his only son. At the time, the Margate second XI, played in the bottom league of the Kent amateur cricket structure; otherwise known as 'Kent Regional League - 2B East'. Now, as you have read, Billy made his noticeable impression on the club three months prior in the April of that year. So, with us not fully understanding his life situation at that point, as anyone would, we took great amusement at Billy's participation in the game!

So, the morning of the game arrived where Billy's not yet named son, was instigating moves to ready himself to make an untimely evacuation from his mother's womb! Not knowing whether he'd even be able to get to the ground for the 1:30pm start; Billy floated around the idea that he may not be able to play. This was accepted by the second team skipper, as anyone playing the first team game could have filled in at the last minute. So, soon enough, 1:30 came around; *"Was Billy going to turn up?"* we all thought. Sure enough, as a game of cricket was involved, of course he did! Billy left the Mother of his first-born child at 1:20pm after she gave birth to him just over two hours before at 10:44am!

Weighing in at healthy six and a half pounds; Dylan Stephen Charles Woollard was born. It does beg the question though! Why on Earth would anyone leave the woman who just passed a human being the size of a watermelon through their legs to go and play cricket? Well, this is something you'll have to ask him; however, I like to think Billy must have felt on for a ton that day! After all, it was a two's game and he did get lucky with the simple fact that his swimmers actually worked in the first place! So a little fortune at the crease would have surely followed?!? Wouldn't it? What an ending to this story that would be!

Did Billy get lucky? No. Did he score his maiden hundred for Margate? Not that day. Did he even make much of a contribution to the game? Somewhat. What Billy achieved in the first six hours of Dylan's time on this great planet we all call home, was that he bowled a solitary over from the pavilion end and went for six runs for no reward; where he then batted at three in the 2nd innings - chasing 110, and scored a well-earned... 12. Margate did; however, go on to win the game and keep their 2015 league hopes alive! So, I suppose there's some cricketing solace to that fateful day!

Nevertheless, it did come to pass that after these events in many conversations while penning these tales, that Dylan's mother actually wanted her sister to be her birthing partner and not Billy. And hence, that is why he made the decision to leave soon after his son's birth; wherein quite comedic fashion, she didn't even turn up to support her sister! Anyway, it must be noted that even though Billy played this game of second XI cricket two hours after his son's birth, and even though he obtained a 'thanks for coming award' in the process. I like to think that with myself knowing Bill for the four years since these events, whereby association, also witness his son Dylan reach the age of four and a half; growing into the cricket lover and enthusiast that he is. I think Dylan would love nothing more than to know that his father 'up-sticked' at the hospital hours after his birth, in pursuit of playing the one game, that not only his dad eternally loves, but he endlessly loves too.

Billy on his Return After Making 12 on Dylan's Birthday *(25/7/15)*

Almost Saved the Day! - 2015

Taking a step back into the world of actually playing cricket, this next tale comes in the form of possibly one of the greatest individual performances of my village cricket career. In August of 2015, we had one of our final league fixtures to date against Littlebourne CC, and boy was it a cracker! Playing at home, chasing 184, we knew this run chase was going to be a somewhat tough endeavour, made even worse by losing our first three wickets for only five runs!

Batting at my, then, usual position of five, I walked to the crease a man who had lost four stone up until that point and, if I'm being honest, was starting to look a bit like a malnourished Ugandan child! Anyway, having been set the task of rescuing the innings by Ian, while also keeping up with the run rate to attain the required runs within the remaining 38 overs, this was never going to be a foregone conclusion! So, in strong agreement with my batting partner, who I believe also hadn't faced a ball by that point, we concurred that to rebuild the innings and take our partnership to at least ten overs would be the best course of action. So, as if Tivoli Meadow had taken a time machine back to the 1970's; I produced a performance for the next eight overs that even Geoffrey Boycott would have been proud of! Scoring roughly one an over for the duration of that time. Harry Brooks; however, at the other end decided that my forward defence masterclass was too good to replicate himself and elected to override the pre-agreed plan by missing an attempted heave to cow corner; losing his off peg in the process!

So, there I was, feeling ready to give the ball a bit of tap in the relatively near future, when the wickets started to tumble; three down quickly became four, and on the face of it, any reasonable chance of securing victory. With us now 13-4 and Ian batting at six that day; a captain's knock was in dire need! Surely my original plan to rescue the innings could still be implemented. As it happens, it did; Ian and I took the score to 94 before his untimely demise! Now five down and into the somewhat competent tail. With a couple of cameos and myself proficiently putting the bad ball away; I soon found myself surpassing fifty. Although this was nice from an individual standpoint, the job was far from complete! So in somewhat parallel comparison to Ben Stokes celebrating his heroic hundred in the 3rd test of the 2019 Ashes; a simple raise of the bat was held to acknowledge my innings thus far, but my head positioned firmly towards the Tivoli Meadow dustbowl; concentrating on the task still in hand. After all, we still needed 60 to win! Even though these cameos were useful, the periodical fall of wickets always kept Littlebourne in the driving seat. They knew however, the game was not won until they saw me physically walk back to the pavilion!

Now, with myself on sixty-odd but the team still needing 40 to win from ten overs; in strolls Dave Price. An ex-army veteran; Colonel in rank, having served 40 years for Queen and country from the age of 16. He had fought in various conflicts from Afghanistan to Northern Ireland; this man fundamentally lived and breathed for pressure. In fact, if one were writing a list as to who could deal with some simple 'village cricket tension', this man would surely be at the top of your list! This apparent belief in the army vet was never in doubt; with evidently his the years of leading precise military expeditions all rushing firmly back into place; where he smashed twenty-odd in as many deliveries! One could have figuratively suspended all bets on an improbable Margate victory after this valuable partnership! We now needed 11 to win from two overs; victory was within grasp! With Colonel Price having met his end, and myself now over 80; having supported the army man's valuable innings; undoubtably reminiscent to the troops going 'over the top', these 11 runs to win were nothing other than within my exclusive custody!

This is, however, where the story comes to a hasty and anticlimactic end. With us now on 176, needing nine to win with only one wicket and six balls remaining; one agricultural moo would have seen us virtually home! One mistake; would have cost us the game. Littlebourne calculatedly utilised my likely thinking and elected to provide a gap at cow corner to facilitate such a farming endeavour. Did I take them up on their offer? Of course I took them up on their generous fielding omission! The fairytale ending prominently projecting from my minds eye was that of sheer dystopian fiction! Where I unsurprisingly found a thick inside edge; allowing myself and Tom to get back for two. Now needing seven from five balls, I opted for round two in my bid for an early harvest. The bowler however, delivered an unexpected plot twist in this nail-biting affair! He bowled a short; wide delivery, which was just back of a length, and in the honest truth, should have been creamed for four through backward point! But as anyone who might be familiar with the particular grounds in the Thanet district area; Margate is the polar opposite to the actual MCC; not a batsman's paradise; but a front foot plodder's dream! As such, playing at this ground for all my formative years; a front foot plodder I became! Consequently, this meant I was not well versed in dispatching short and wide gifts! I subsequently produced the thickest of thick outside edges and looped the ball right into the bucket like hands of the strategically placed fielder at fly-slip! The game - was over. We had lost.

After falling foul to the rank long-hop; we were all out; losing the game by six runs. So close! But yet so far! With myself entering the crease at 5 for 3, to mishitting that final delivery for a well-earned but futile 85; Littlebourne were right, they would win the game when they saw the back of me. It just so happened to be that they also saw the side of me as we walked off the field in agonising collective unison! Still, I can take great satisfaction in the fact that Littlebourne went on to win the league that year, and carried on winning their respective divisions every year since. So, to not only put a performance in against them, in not only this game, but also in other matches before their emphatic rise in the Kent amateur cricket structure. I think is something to be greatly proud of.

TALES OF THE ONE AND ONLY MCC ADULT CRICKET TOUR - 2015

After a year of great weight loss and losing over four stone in 12 months; the August bank holiday weekend of 2015 was certainly one to remember! With an emerging new-found confidence and a great set of mates who generally understood my social deficiencies, we had the opportunity to spend an extra night of tour before everyone else. We'd have be silly not to! I digress though; as this tour to Kingston-upon-Themes had a substantive amount of memorable tales, it has been split up into four stories full of trains, drunkenness, dying (yes, dying) and of course, a shit game of cricket!

1) CULTURE AND UNCOUTHNESS ON A LOCOMOTIVE

To begin this narrative of life-changing events, our first story begins on the Friday before the August bank holiday weekend, on the train from Ramsgate to New Cross. Writing this in 2019, in what is now a well-rehearsed agenda for trips away, Billy proposed the then, innovative idea that instead of a two-day weekend tour, we should take the opportunity to venture into the place where he spent the majority of his formative years before meeting up with the team on the Saturday. We thought it would be a great idea! We wouldn't have to worry about cricket club politics, and it would be a good starting point to springboard future antics for the next two days! Well — at least this was the idea!

So, there we were; myself, Brett, Billy, James and Dan all ready to embark on this trip of a lifetime. I obviously brought along wine and nibbles for the somewhat lengthy excursion! I had a great time; there was a real air of class surrounding the whole occasion. This was until Billy removed his rucksack from his back, unzipped the top, and proceeded to reveal a full-size bottle of Jack Daniels whiskey and an abundance of full-fat coke cola! My pre-conceived idea of how this trip was going to unravel, had evidently taken a clear and abrupt U-turn!

So, there we were, enjoying the two-hour journey from Thanet to London; music blaring; drinking games in full obnoxious swing; certain individuals illegally vaping, ticket officers turning blind eyes to all of this; and the five of us in the middle of a deserted train carriage having a great time! However, some of us more than others. It became quickly apparent that while I had my fair share of fermented red grapes, Billy unsurprisingly, and if I'm being honest, comprehensively inhaled the entire contents of his once full

My Idea of Train Drinking

bottle of JD. If I remember; he distinctly had great trouble stringing a coherent sentence together; not even being able to articulate his own name, let alone shepherd the rest of us to his nan's house a short walk from the tube station! This caused great alarm for me and the rest of the early tourists, as we were in the middle of London with not a bloody clue of where his nan lived! This consequently, has the severe knock-on implication of not having the foggiest inclination of where we would be sleeping that night! Ready to accept our unavoidable fate, we thought it would be best to take stock, have some dinner in Weatherspoons and hope that Bill could sober up to guide us through this final, and most crucial first leg of the tour.

Billy's idea...

Time soon passed with us all sat in the middle of the pub, having acknowledged our immediate futures of temporary homelessness in the capital; where a miracle happened! After numerous pints of water, a chicken burger and a quick visit to the gents to freshen up; Billy finally recalled the address where he spent the first 18 years of his life! I will never forget the words that suddenly emerged from his mayonnaise-covered mouth, *"28 Cranston Road!"* he exclaimed! We were saved! No longer did we have to entertain the thought of a cold, uncomfortable night, and probably were prevented from adding ourselves to London's rampant rise of knife crime victims! We weren't going to die! Or, so I thought...

2) VENUE NIGHT CLUB

W hat you are about to read in the next two memoirs are probably the most important, pivotal and influential moments of my life. Up until this point in late August of 2015, I had devoted so much time to cricket; what it stood for; the prestige, the culture; the values and the beliefs. These were the nights where I, Josh Williamson, stood in the face of an engrained parental ideology that 'loud night clubs were the spawn of Satan and should be avoided at all costs'. These were the nights where I, Josh Williamson, died and became a changed man.

As was always the plan from the thought of conception for the 2015 tour, an unofficial first night at Venue night club in New Cross was on the agenda. This was Billy's teenage hunting ground; effectively his home from home, and boy was it a grand homecoming! After at long last, gaining refuge at Bill's nan's house, we set ourselves up in the various rooms within the gaff. Billy was obviously sleeping in his juvenile dwelling; Brett and Dan were sharing; myself in his dad's old room and James on the sofa. After the necessary tour of the London pad, Billy showed us the contents of his old bedside draw, to which in a personal gift to myself, provided me with a full packet of condoms and an assortment of flavoured lubes; just in case I struck lucky and ended my 21-year drought of non-solo sexual activity! So, after swift storage of the wondrous trinkets, it was soon time to ready ourselves for the first night to end all nights!

The taxi promptly arrived, at a reasonably late hour of 10pm, and dropped us off outside the club. This was not before the smokers of the group wisely procuring themselves of cigarettes and other implements to ensure exiting the nocturnal club would not be required halfway through the night. Although I didn't smoke, this was for everyone else, and let's be honest, I wasn't going to be standing by myself in the middle of London, waiting to be mugged now was I?!? Well, as it happens, I probably would have been better off actioning that plan! Upon departing the off-license and ambling towards the club, we were unexpectedly greeted by a homeless man requesting some loose change. Bill, without hesitation, stormed off; providing the rationale that he only carries card. But as if I was a rabbit in a blinding headlight; I submitted to this 'persuasive' request for money from the dishevelled un-sheltered man! Quite frankly, at the time I had the somewhat irrational and compelling urge to maintain my vital organs in all their entirety! I mean, the man could have been in a suit and I still would have yielded to this ailing life circumstance! So, I offered an inconsequential sum of

£1, which certainly appeased my perceived potential mugger, and hence, was free to make quick haste in catching up with William and the boys' to start off the night properly

Walking across the road, with the rest of the lads already in the club, I could feel my heart beating out of my chest! Something was dreadfully wrong. Then it occurred to me, this was the first time I had ever been in a night club! Everything was going through my head. What was going to happen? How crowded is it going to be? Am I going to meet girls? What do I say? What if they like me? Do I kiss them? What if they kiss me? There was so much uncertainty! Everything was clearly brand new and the night's events so unknown, that even though I didn't think much of it at the time, it makes perfect sense now. After handing over my £5 entrance fee to the broadly set doorman and crept slowly downstairs; holding both hands strangling the rail bar. I was finally able to join the rest of the boys' at the front of the bar where we ordered our first round of drinks. I knew something really wasn't right, but I couldn't put my finger on it; I simply shrugged it off as probably just my nerves and a drink would soon sort it! To evidently provide some much-needed rest bite for my increasingly faster and faster beating heartbeat, I asked Brett to check my pulse to check that it wasn't just me. He quickly put his fingers on my wrist, 15 seconds passed and Brett replied,

"No Josh, you're fine mate, chill".

"Phew" I thought, *"just me".*

Some more minutes passed; my heart was still in overdrive! With Dan overhearing my significant and overwhelming concerns for my personal welfare, he 'wisely' provided copious amounts of additional vodka laced with Red Bull to remedy this precarious situation. What was his reasoning for such a resolution I hear you ask? Well, apparently the justification must have been that speeding up one's heart even further could do nothing other than slow it down! I inhaled the drink like I had just spent 40 days in the Sharjah Desert, it was not unlike to the events of Bill's previous exploits with the JD on the train! Still worried, I exclaimed;

> *"Brett, it's still crazy, I need an ambulance, call an ambulance –*
> *NOW!"*

With Brett clearly not knowing what to do, he pondered the situation, started to turn away as if he was conceding to my demands, and then — THUD! As if I was like Del-Boy in 'Only Fools and Horses', I collapsed in front of the bar of the night club's hard-wooden floor; providing no external support whatsoever to break my fall. What happened next, I only became aware of later due to a selection of eye-witness accounts the next morning, but all I remember is that I befriended the Venue nightclub floor in a rather expedient fashion, and remained good friends with it for quite some time!

While lying is this comatose state on the floor, I heard accounts that everyone in the bar thought I had actually died! Time stood still for Dan who thought he had killed me by naïvely supplying numerous of unneeded energy drinks mixed with alcohol. Apparently, the barmaid simply didn't care; physically stepping over me to deliver empty glasses to the bar. Billy was apparently in the corner of the room providing reassurance to the twitchy bouncer who was clearly eager to evict me from the premises. While also, using these events for his future self's possible self-gratification; chatting up two girls, one of whom from this point will be named 'Venue Sophie'. All while Brett positioned me into the recovery position as he was the closest to my horizontal resting place!

These are the events that actually happened while all this was going on. I on the other hand, was envisaging throwing the winning touchdown in the super bowl! I don't know why, I don't even really like American football, so why this was my thought construct, I'll never know! I was calling all the plays, making some useful distance with each attacking drive that started on my own goal line. Where finally, as if it was something out of the film 'Waterboy', with my team down on points with ten seconds to go in the 4th quarter; I threw this last-ditch Hail Mary from the fifty-yard line to my wide receiver, where he dived; caught the ball, scored the touchdown and won the Super Bowl! As soon as that catch was made, I resurrected from my universally agreed death, to the sound of Brett and Dan, *"Josh, are you ok, are you ok?"* Billy didn't want to necessarily know that, he barged through the circling Venue crown, grabbed my hand, pulled me up and marched me directly out into the smoking area to allow me to recover in the fresh air. We stayed there for must have been a good three hours, talking about those events over and over again. About how I won the Super Bowl; how I was passed out for only three minutes but felt like an American football games length, and why on earth I envisaged these things. Maybe it was a past life, maybe it was a future life, maybe — it was my way of going towards the light, no one will ever know. How I didn't get thrown out is also a complete and utter mystery, suppose it was probably Bill's knowledge of particular doormen that assisted with that quandary. But for the rest of the night, it was like the once shy and timid boy, who gave money to innocent homeless men because he thought they were dangerous, morphed into this personality that could talk to girls once introduced, was content in a night club and could finally, finally, hold some level of competence in social situations when in the company of his supporting mates!

Because of these happenings, we actually talked to Venue Sophie and co, for the rest of that night, I think I even got a kiss! I didn't, however, get to make use of Billy's previous donation, but it was a start! As such, let it be known here, that at this stage of my social development, this was the night where my voyage of life began to take a starboard turn in an entirely different direction!

Pictures of that night in Venue

3) THE FORK IN THE ROAD

With the 2015 tour now fully underway and my resurrection complete, the Saturday morning after we promptly made our way across London to our temporary accommodation for the remaining two nights, at the Travelodge in Kingston. As some certain parties elected to stay at home at the last moment, this left an extra bedroom for a couple of lucky organised people; these fortunate people happened to be none other than myself and my father! This did however, cause a rather sizeable surge of uproar with two particular tour-goers, as clearly they wanted their own individual sleeping arrangements! Nevertheless, Dad and I 'artfully' gave a figurative 'up-yours' to the prospective room-poaching parties and countered their abject disapproval by hastily unpacking all our belongings into the minimally furnished hotel rooms! The Williamson's would not be moved!

If I distinctly remember, Wetherspoons was also the unofficial caterer for Margate's reverse jolly boys' outing, as I believe we opted for breakfast, lunch and dinner in nationwide chain for the entire tour! Anyway, with myself and Dad now controversially set-up in our adjacent, but completely separate living quarters, it was unanimously decided by the team that venturing out into London after a quick bite to eat was the only way one could spend the first official night! Again, Spoons was first on the list;

burger and chips all round. After seeing off our modestly-priced meals, we quickly realised that this was not any ordinary Spoons; it was a Wetherspoons — with music! The tables were punctually reorganised as the clock stuck 9pm to reveal a dance floor! What even was this? A dance floor at Spoons! It wasn't anything any of us had ever encountered before, less notably me! Shots and Jäger bombs soon followed, before it was eventually time to make haste towards Clapham Grand night club via the tube, which from memory, some of us didn't pay for, including myself!

So, with the below-ground locomotive soon reaching its desired end, and myself with no ticket to present the London Transport Police if requested. We walked towards the exit to be greeted, to a ticket barrier and, you guessed it; a couple of Train Policemen! I was quite literally bricking it! What was I going to do? How on Earth could I get through the exit point and evade the police? Thinking I was going to be spending the rest of my days as a wanted fugitive, I was luckily saved by a few of the teammates who did legitimately pay for the public service! We simply stuck closely behind them while negotiating our way through the barrier to remedy one of my disproportionately neurotic concerns. Now, all we had to do was get past the eagle-eyed Rozzas', who quite clearly saw our little misdemeanour. With myself now sweating like a lamb lining up for slaughter, I was told to walk slowly and calmly as we neared the police at the exit; making sure we smiled on our way through, to not give the game away. Somehow, it worked! They smiled back and we were free! No one was getting arrested; no one was spending time in Her Majesty's pleasure; everyone could enjoy the rest of the night!

It was a fairly lengthy walk to the night club from memory, transiting past the Church of Nazarene that had a large over-arching sign titled 'Jesus'; providing no doubt what the purpose of the building was for. Clearly, after the previous night's events surrounding my untimely death and subsequent resurrection, the most obvious, and probably grossly distasteful, photo opportunity presented itself! So, with myself arranging my limbs in the universally acknowledged shape of Jesus on the crucifix; my arms held out to the side and feet fixed together. Josh, A.K.A 'Jesus', was reborn! After enjoying this controversial fun a little too much, Clapham Grand was finally in sight! It wasn't too busy for London and we quickly gained entry, paid our £10 to the lady and procured ourselves a drink to properly kick things off! Not wanting anything too heavy, Gin and Tonic was my poison of choice. I know London is expensive, but they cost £7.50! SEVEN POUNDS AND FIFTY PENCE for a sodding single Gin and Tonic! I wasn't too happy, but with no option other than to sober up, I was left with little choice but to imbibe in this most unmistakable display of night-time extortion! It also didn't help the fact that the bloody drink was blue to the naked eye; even thinking I was spiked in conjunction with being required to take a second mortgage out! Well — technically first mortgage! But you get the sentiment.

So, after ten minutes under the roof of this establishment that we had effectively carried out a pilgrimage to reach. While in the toilets emptying my alcohol-filled bladder in the next but one urinal to Ant, he eluded to the fact that he didn't like this loud club and was planning on heading back to the hotel; inviting me in the process as my dad would be nothing apart from worried sick. I calculated my options; did I stay or did I go? Where I concluded that I also didn't really like the price of the drinks, it was getting busier by the minute and so, I began the process of joining Ant and company. As I was swiftly saying my goodbyes to the remaining clubbers, Billy pulled my left arm abruptly back just as I transition towards the exit foyer threshold, asked *"Where the fuck was I was going?"*, and promptly summarised the full context of the previously abridged choices that were presented only moments earlier. Quoting;

> *"Josh, you can go home, be boring and never be a real man. Or you can stay, have fun and enjoy more of what we did last night at Venue".*

This focused the easily impressionable mind of my 21-year-old self. I didn't want to be boring, I really enjoyed last night and wanted to do it again! I was beginning to feel something I had never felt in my life before! I was beginning to feel 'normal'.

Admittedly this was one contributing factor, and if I'm being honest, I wanted better value for my £10 entrance fee! At that point, we had effectively paid a pound a minute! Anyway, what could really go wrong? After all, I died not even 24 hours previously! So, with myself standing in the club's well-lit foyer, weighing up the streamlined menu of available conclusions, the decision to stay in Clapham and build upon the previous night's developments was emphatically chosen!

After a few of these hyper-inflated blue beverages, it was wasn't long before the remaining tour clubbers' were in discussion with a couple of lovely young ladies, one of whom I shall call for the remainder of this story as, 'Posh Bird'. Now, Posh Bird was something else! I think I quite literally fell in love for the first time that night! So, after exchanging pleasantries with her, Bill clearly became jealous of my somewhat evident string of autism induced successes, and began to move his right index finger towards the general vicinity of Posh Bird's anus! Shouting rather loudly the phrase *"BUM HOLE!"* as it graduated closer and closer towards the landing zone! The purpose of this legally-questionable act was in pursuit of interrogating why on earth she was talking to me of all people! After all, I was autistic! A distinct yelp erupted from her mouth; repositioned her right hand firmly across Billy's face, and eloquently told him to *"Foxtrot Oscar!"* I evidently apologised for my friend and explained that he can be a right 'so and so' sometimes. This was accepted by her and we enjoyed a fair few dances in close, side-by-side proximity! I only say a 'fair few' and nothing more, as while in the process of this comprehensive display of adjacent 'Dad' dancing, I got a little too carried away; carelessly bopping my head back and forth far too vigorously, where I — nutted Posh Bird in her pretty little forehead right into next week! She lost her footing; forcefully pushed me away and told me I could also now *"Foxtrot Oscar!"* She unsurprisingly held her hand over her nose, to which I can only assume was because I caused a nosebleed! I shat myself! So, in not quite knowing what to do, I said sorry and ran away like a little girl back to my nearby-observing mates; never seeing Posh Bird again!

Although this evening didn't quite go to plan. I, again, stood in the face of sensible reasoning. Where I think if I were to take a step back from this story and look at myself now in 2019. That the decision to stay in that nightclub while standing in the foyer of Clapham Grand, is, if I'm being perfectly frank, the biggest fork in my road of life to date. Bigger than deciding to go to uni; larger than opting to play cricket at the age of nine; heck, the gravity of that decision was probably on par with the choice made for me back in 1993, when my mother and father thought unprotected sexual intercourse nine months before my birth would be a good idea! I often think, that if I had listened to my head and joined Ant on his woeful retreat back to the hotel, would I have this story to tell? Would I have any stories to tell for that matter? Would I have the confidence to talk to the opposite sex? Would I even be friends with the group of mates I practically call family? I think the emphatic answer to all those philosophical quandaries is, no.

The Chosen Path down the Fork in the Road

I think the events of that night in Clapham, and Venue, were quite simply the catalyst for who I am today. It built the foundations of confidence to allow me to remain socially buoyant in a heavily female dominated university cohort, which happened to start two weeks after these experiences! I think if I were to

pinpoint my academic successes while at uni in the years since, that without those two character-forming nights', starting that significant chapter at university in September of 2015 would have been practically impossible given my neurological impairments! Which, ultimately, without those four years of higher education, I would not be enjoying the rewards of my achievements today! To put it bluntly, without cricket and the opportunities being involved in the game that is has presented me, I would be hating my life, earning ten grand a year as a teaching assistant, and crucially, still weird and completely socially inept.

It was Blue; Honest!!

Jesus!!

No Idea?!!

Posh Bird!! (Next to me)

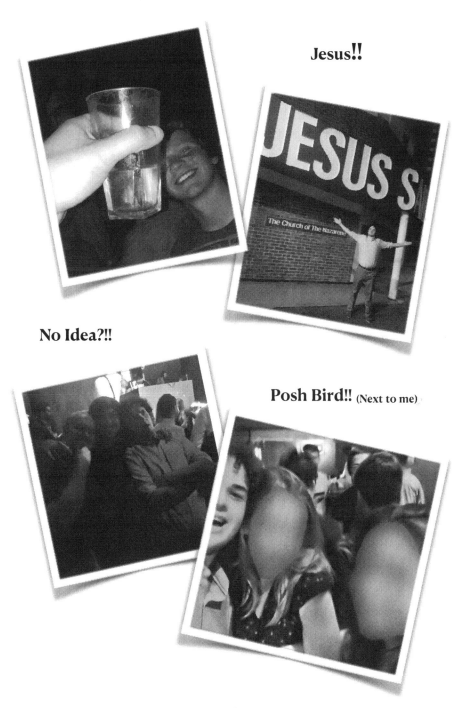

4) THE HORRIFIC GAME

To finish this section surrounding the 2015 tour, it is now time to actually bring up some cricket! As it happened, this was the only game played because the Monday after was a complete washout! Having said that, this story does centre around a rainy and very cold game vs Magdalen CC at Imber Court! Nevertheless, after the heavy nights before, while electing to bat first, it was decided by Ian that the two victims chosen to open the batting should also be the two people most hungover and, probably, still drunk! This honour categorically went to Dan Carter and Brett Kirk! With myself not wanting to go anywhere near the crease with the willow in hand, and consequently stare 22-yards away from death; so I reserved number 11. As a result, for the early overs, I enthusiastically volunteered my officiating services; donned a helmet, grabbed the figurative popcorn and witness the proceeding events unravel from the best seat in the house! So, with myself now equipped with Bill's yellow lid navigating both Brett and Dan taking their guards, what happened next you couldn't predict! Well — you probably could. Yes, predictably, there was this left-armer who couldn't bowl much quicker than 50mph having Brett and Dan in all sorts of trouble! Anything outside the off stump resulted in a guaranteed play and miss. Anyone that's tried to bat hungover, or still under the influence, knows full well of the struggle you are just about to read!

In adding to the fortunes of the opening duo, the only thing that could provide any level of much-needed rest bite between comprehensively shifting Oxygen particles, was when they were both getting pinned firmly to the crease ball after ball! Hitting them far too many times to count! As I'm sure you can imagine, they were playing this guy like Steve Harmison in his 2005 Ashes prime, and still even then, when they tried to commit batting suicide to end their miserable existence at the crease, they couldn't even achieve that! Consequently, rum was supplied at periodic intervals, in the form of unofficial drinks breaks; ensuring sobering up was not an option for the two struggling openers! I think these two learned a lesson that day — bat 11!

I must unfortunately say, this is probably the only decent thing to happen in that game. For the remainder, we were subjected to rain, cold, a barely passable tea, and the sight of their opener taking us to the cleaners with a 32 ball fifty! Still though, to provide some light consolation, Brett and Dan did come off the field like they had both finished 12 rounds with Mike Tyson! So it wasn't a complete waste of time!

Anyway, we limped to the score of 144, with myself achieving a solid three from seven, batting at 11. Before it was our turn to withstand the wet and freezing London field. For whatever reason, Ant imposed a 'dick head' mask for me to wear while wicket keeping. It could have been something to do with me throwing a tennis ball at the back of his head, but I didn't think it warranted that. Most likely, it had something to do with my U-turn of not joining him on his £1 a minute stay in Clapham night club! Nevertheless, Chris Carter; our chairman, bowled the first ball, which surprisingly was actually pretty good! Where after that procession, we were all essentially turkeys' yearning for Christmas; no one wanted to be there; we all wanted to start the 3rd night of shenanigans! But no! Because it was a 'cricket tour' we had to play actual cricket! Soon after their opener's sending of multiple missiles, our suffering was finally ended! We could at long last enter the abattoir; our heads could be been cut off; it was over! We had lost the game but finally, finally, could enjoy our metaphorical Christmas Dinner!

Our Chairman, Chris Carter, Bowling the First Ball while I was Keeping in my New 'Hat'

BRETT'S 30TH - 2016

As we near closer and closer towards the present, 2016 was a great year to resume my newfound confidence within social circles and renewed lease for life. After concluding a first successful term at university in the latter months of 2015; this year started with a bang! In January of 2016, one of my best mates Brett, the same chair invader at the Eurovision party some months earlier, finally turned 30. So with that unavoidable milestone happening, he hosted a house party at his new home in Ramsgate. All the usual suspects at the cricket club were invited, including Mum and Dad. Beer pong had been set up; the chairs were intricately placed to make best use of the adequately sized lounge-diner area, and the summertime garden furniture conveniently was dusted off to facilitate a bespoke setting for the smokers among us. Due to my new lease of confidence and compelling willingness to defy my own mother's ingrained expectations for me when growing up; I took up a six-month sabbatical to imbibe in smoking socially when enjoying a few drinks. She, at this point, did not know of this miscalculated life decision, and as such, due to her presence at this shindig, I was forced to tiptoe around the figurative ice to fully enjoy my ill-thought-out social imperatives! Needless to say, it was a great party! My mother conducted her usual behaviours of 'faking' her inebriation, even playing beer pong with Brett's mum; Barbara. Together, mine and Brett's initial reaction portrayed thoughts that this occurrence is something that only happens in the film, American Pie! We couldn't quite comprehend the events unfolding in front of our very eyes! I'm not sure who won, but please take my word, it was a sight to behold! Two fifty-something women playing a drinking game, with both their son's present, observing every throw of the ball; amazing!

**Mum vs Brett's Mum
at Beer Pong!**

Nonetheless, I, once again, had a little too much to drink and quietly retired up to my then claimed bedroom at Brett's gaff at around midnight to sleep off my enthusiastic display of consuming alcoholic beverages. This, however, is where my night took a slight turn for the worse! Three hours elapsed; I woke up from my drunk slumber to the sounds of Brett's 30th still in full flow.

Although, I do not remember what happened, I have it documented via two video graphic sources, that with myself wearing nothing more than my boxers, I ventured downstairs to scope out what was happening. As it turned out, not a lot, until I made my unambiguous entrance! While stumbling down the tightly woven staircase, I saw JP. Where completely out of my normal character, gave him a one-armed cuddle, and he promptly suggested that I returned to sleep. I most predictably declined that invitation. What happened next, again, one could not possibly script or imaginatively conjure up for fictitious purposes! I heard the comment that the diameter of my nipples were larger than a normal male! This could be because my man boobs were quite large when I was fat and thus is probably one side effect of rectifying my adolescent issues of morbid obesity. Where, again, I heard the re-occurring advice that it would be best for my physical, and mental, wellbeing that a prompt return to bed would be the best course of action. I clearly, did not take kindly to this advice, and swiftly called the contributors of the unwarranted counsel that they were all *"Hitler"*. Ok, I hear you saying, this isn't exactly original, calling people who tell other humans what to do *"Hitler"*, isn't exactly an original comment. However, after salmon diving on the most persistent informant, while wearing nothing but my underpants, I conceded and unconvincingly began to make my way back up the stairs. As I reached the sharp corner on the staircase mid-section, Brett proceeded to ask me how much I had that night; clearly I didn't have the foggiest idea! So, building upon my previous knowledge of World War Two figureheads, I proceeded to call him *"Starling"*.

"Who the fuck is Starling?" Brett questioned.

Clearly, this was an unintended mispronunciation of the communist Soviet dictator! I understand that I additionally supported my historical claim via the use of further unmentionable expletives and tarred the birthday boy with the same historical travesties! Ultimately, I didn't remember a thing until the morning after where I was enlightened of the events via video footage on the Facebook group chat for all the members to see in its witty glory!

"Starling!"

Oh 2016, what a year! The stories keep getting better and better! I continue my series of anecdotical cricket-themed memoirs in the form of Brett's stag do to Cardiff in the April. As I delve into the events of that fateful trip, I must note that although it could be perceived to be fiction, I can completely confirm, it is not.

1) DID SHE DIE?

With a large contingent of cricket personnel forming the vast majority of Brett's stag party, we, much like in the 2015 tour, rendezvoused at Ramsgate train station and set course for Cardiff Central. This trip rings so many similarities to the excursion to Kingston; Billy wielded another bottle of JD and myself with wine, but big bottles this time! Vaping on the train! It's so similar, it's uncanny! The only difference was that we were required to carry a full set of golf clubs, as it was planned to play on an Open Championship qualifier course in between the nighttime antics! I must admit, it was a mission! An hour and a half to London, a short trip on the tube, then four hours to Cardiff; it was a long haul of locomotive drinking, but we did it! A taxi was then called to get to our hotel in what felt like the middle of the Welsh valleys, where Dan was asleep for the whole car ride. Eventually, we met up with the rest of the stag party to commence the first planned night of three.

Night one, we didn't know where to go in the centre of Cardiff, so clearly, I had no hope! Eventually, it was posited that a bar called Live Lounge was the 'go-to' place in the city. It's marketed as a bar that plays live music for 12 hours a day, seven days a week. In my rather inexperienced opinion, it was certainly lively! Happy hour lasted from 6pm till 11pm, so in reality, it was happy five hours; however, this only increased the fun we had! So, there we were, dancing away to whatever musical genre the bar organised that Wednesday night. Where this gremlin looking female made her acquaintance to our group. We all offered pleasantries, where subsequently she, to my reluctant surprise held my hand; called me *"Gorgeous"* and proceeded to dance in a somewhat persuasive fashion; focusing much of her attention towards my pelvic region! I didn't quite know what to do, so this continued for a while, before evidently, she had one too many drinks for her constitution to handle, where she, in parallel fashion to myself at Venue the year prior, collapsed headfirst and face planted the floor! None of her friends were to be seen to rescue the situation, unlike myself eight months before! I must admit, I then exhibited pretty poor gentlemanly form by slowly reversing back into the circling Live Lounge crowd! Although, not my proudest moment, I escaped with my freedom! If I'm being honest, I thought she died, and the blame would be pointed solely towards me! She survived though as we saw her not even thirty minutes later in the smoking area clearly seeking for an alternative male's bed to sleep in!

2) THE FIRST SIGHTING OF FEMALE GENITALIA!

After that culture shock of being on the other foot when someone else collapsed, it was suggested that no stag do was complete without a visit to a strip club! So, without hesitation, we utilised Brett's well-developed internet surfing skills where he located the existence of not one; not two; but three strip clubs in Cardiff! And the best thing was, all three were on the same street!

So, with google maps directing our somewhat lengthy trek to see boobies, and myself not having a clue where we were; we eventually made our way to the Pleasure Palace. It wasn't actually called that, but for the interest of privacy, I thought it would be best to change the name. Anyway, after supporting this gentlemen's club by subscribing to their £5 entrance fee, we ventured upstairs while also being read the riot act as to the establishment's strict rules. While listening intently to the obvious regulations, we were directed to the VIP section, as quite frankly it was dead in there, and we said it was Brett's stag do. So, there we were, in the close approximal company of two lovely young, self-employed ladies, having a few beers, where one by one, the boys' were escorted to the various private booths to enjoy personal demonstrations of the female figure. Obviously, with myself now sitting there on my lonesome, being autistic and never having experienced a situation like this before, let alone seeing a naked woman 1st hand, I can clearly remember the compelling rationale swirling through my head;

"Josh, you've never seen a pair of boobs before apart from your own mother's, this is your time to shine!"

Now, I was sitting there in the intimate company of the one stripper's name I actually remember; Beth. So, to ease the obvious tension building up; while not knowing quite what to say or how to act, I abruptly uttered this most memorable phrase;

"Suppose it's time to see your boobs then".

It appeared Beth the stripper liked this most unintendedly forward and blunt gesture; swiftly directing me into one of the booths the rest of the boys' were so keen to enter previously! Before I knew it, the music had started! I must be honest at this point, that although it is probably universally known that strippers reenact the female version of the Full Monty, I was not eluded to this rather important and pertinent fact at the time. So, there I was, quite literally bricking it with nerves as to what she was doing to do.

"Was she going to touch my penis?"

"Was she going to put her boobs in my face?"

"Do I even say anything to her?"

As it happened, I shouldn't have worried at all! In the only way I really knew how, I sparked, 'light' conversation with Beth the stripper -

"Do you enjoy your job?"

"Why do you do subject yourself to this?"

"Are your parents proud of you?"

With Beth evidently really quite shocked and not knowing what to say or how to react; other than reply with words, she retorted with actions to hush the mouth of this obvious autistic boy. She firstly removed her strapless bra, that I'm pretty sure had an overly worn and well-used clasp, due to the frequent removal of the said piece of clothing; and proceeded to gyrate her hips in a somewhat suggestive manner! To be honest, I was happy with simply that; I had seen a pair of boobs and I was satisfied, *"£20 well spent!"* I thought. But in the now obvious retrospective surprise, more clothing was being removed! Her thong was now around her ankles!

"Wow!" I thought.

"I don't believe my naively minded luck! This has made my year, and we're only in April!"

I had finally seen my first vagina other than on the way out of my mother's uterus 21 years ago!

So, as with all good things, the dance abruptly came to a sudden conclusion; I had the best four minutes of my life; even better than my maiden hundred! On re-admittance into the public lounge area, I was greeted to the Cheshire Cat like smiling faces of my best mates; Brett and Billy et al! They knew full well that this was a first experience in my sheltered life. This reaction was additionally supported by the obvious 'tent-like' structure emitting from my blue corduroy trousers! Billy enjoyed his time so much, I'm pretty sure he emphatically fell in love with Beth the stripper, as he joined her for many more visitations; spending an ungodly amount of money! Even requesting my expedited hunt for a nearby cash machine utilising his bank card to fund his comprehensive selection of the extravagant 'À la carte' menu of services from his new stripper love! I must admit, that especially after this experience, even though I was confident as to where my sexuality was situated from early teenage hood; I just simply lacked the core interpersonal competencies to act upon it. That this encounter only confirmed my long believed biological deductions! Simply put, could this day have got any better?

As it happened, it could! Although what you are thinking didn't happen; that's a story for another day. But on the inherently wise decision to procure ourselves of a 4th McDonald's within 24 hours, I saw Beth and her fellow self-employed clothes remover! Even though they clearly tried to quiet my enthusiastic sighting in the adjacent fast food outlet; I made it abundantly obvious that yes, I had indeed spotted our newly acquainted, vagina-showing sub-contractors! Clearly, only I would utilise the technicality that we were no longer under the strict rules and regulations of the Pleasure Palace, and so, in the only way I really knew how, innocently requested a photograph of the first woman that was kind enough to share with me a first-hand experience of female genitalia.

Beth the Stripper

Not Beth the Stripper...

3) THE SUICIDAL THOUGHT-PROVOKING TRIP HOME

We had our fun; I'd seen a vagina 1st hand, and it was soon time to go home to our increasingly louder and louder calls for our own beds in Thanet. This trip home was, to say the least, the worst experience of my life. Worse than the pre-pubescent striding; worse than losing the semi final at Horsham, and although I clearly jest, nothing quite like this experience from Cardiff to Ramsgate has invoked such dire thoughts of jumping in front of an incoming train, or slitting one's wrists and sitting in a bath; simply put, this was horrendous.

Evidently after a third evening of late nights, early mornings, or should I more accurately say, 'early mornings, early mornings' of drinking, it was time to collect our things and set course to return from whence we came; Thanet. To put you into the picture, evidently, we were all severely hungover, sleep-deprived and set the unenviable task of making it home safely with three large and sizeable bags; our suitcase, a rucksack and an awkward to carry set of golf clubs. Due to the excess of self-imposed necessary luggage, this was quite frankly the catalyst to the horror show of a journey home from hell!

The 1st stop for these six fully grown men was getting to Cardiff Central train station via a taxi. This was obviously full of complications; from packing each taxi like some tiny clown car with six clowns inside, to ensuring we allowed enough time to unpack said rides to make the desired train home. Having said that, I suppose the clown car anecdote was actually quite accurate! Anyway, we made it; stage one of three complete. I can hear you all thinking, how on earth did six men all carrying three excessively large bags, find space on the train without causing a public outrage? Well, to be honest, it was a miracle. Finding the required number of seats was a challenge in itself but locating sufficient luggage space nearby to ensure our belongings were safe was virtually impossible! The train gods; however, looked favourably upon these weary passengers; finding six seats and the attached criteria with somewhat relative ease. The only issue we found was that our golf clubs were blocking the disabled access; whereby quite clearly, a sign of 'no baggage in front' was also displayed. We were all thinking;

> *"For the love of God, please don't there be a person in a wheelchair, please!"*

Fortunately for us, the train deities again held us in high regard that day and bestowed upon this returning stag party a first-leg home without a disabled person in sight!

Thinking we were in the clear with this logistical concern, next we had the matter of the train conductor! We sighted the ticket lady early from the far end of the adjacent carriage! To be honest, we were expecting the worst by being forced to move along with our cargo of bags! As she carefully crossed the threshold between the carriages, she was abruptly greeted by a fortification of suitcases and golf clubs blocking any passage! I mean, it was something comparable to the wall in Game of Thrones! She then proceeded to look left; she then looked right, and lastly, made eye-contact with the six of us individually; all of whom had comprehensively surrendered to their temporary self-inflicted misery! Fortunately for us, she expelled a huge sigh of exhaustion; implying that this was not a battle she was prepared to fight, and subsequently turned in the opposite direction to clearly call time on her futile inspection of train tickets.

Now we were over that significant hurdle, and safely in the English Capital city. Our next task was to negotiate the tube across London to St Pancreas International train station, to ultimately secure our safe transit home. In the process of making this perilous trip while carrying the three large bags, we were subjected to many flights of stairs and bumps. This inherently caused physical exhaustion to lug our baggage quietly. I evidently had my rucksack on my back, so that problem was easily dealt with. The golf clubs were also uncomfortably hoisted over my left shoulder, so issue number two was overcome. The suitcase however, proved a step too far for one man to rectify. With my red cabin-sized suitcase held in my right hand on its wheels; carting it along the floor created a new, possibly life-threatening, consequence for this hungover 21-year-old man. The resulting clatter it produced every single footstep; every stair; over every un-even paving stone in London was nothing other than offensive to the ears of anyone in my close proximity! To support your understanding of the noise protruding from this case; whenever I moved it made an increasingly grating and infuriating racket! Only made worse by our hangovers, all we could hear was; thud, thud; thud; *walk down the tube stairs*; thud; thud; *get on the tube*; thud; *get off the tube*; thud; *walk up the stairs*; thud; thud; thud... Obviously, I wasn't aware of the possible ramifications of this unavoidable noise; however, it appeared that everyone else was thinking the same. Billy and Dan were the first to inevitably crack;

> *"Josh, if you don't fucking pick that fucking suitcase up, I'm going to throw you in front the fucking train we are about to get on!"*

I was now evidently in a situation where not only did I want to throw myself in front of the said high-speed train; but everyone else did too! Although clearly, I didn't want to die and obviously wanted to see another day of drinking and strip clubs with my best friends — as well as play cricket! I was however, very tempted to test this bold declaration. Did I test? Of course I did! And, to let you into a little secret; I survived. I was admittedly pretty worried about the welfare of my medium-sized carry case; however, we all made it safely home two hours later, and rather miraculously, all my belongings did too!

The Only Way to Describe Our Trip Home: The Living Dead

TEAM NIGHT - 2016

After a rocky first half to the 2016 cricket season, Brett as the then, first team vice captain, decided to invite the entire playing membership of Margate cricket club for a July house party with the sole purpose to boost a wavering team morale. This social gathering will forever in time and memorial be colloquially endeared to as 'Team Night'. To provide some general context to this team bonding evening, this was scheduled for a Friday night, which, if I'm being perfectly honest, wasn't the wisest of decisions as it was evidently before the Saturday league game! So, there we were enjoying this warm summers night; myself adding my typical air of class to the event by facilitating the opening of half a case of cava; cigarettes and cigars were smoked; and as it happened, so was Billy's place in the first team for the foreseeable future!

I say 'smoked', as quite frankly Billy was chosen to play for the first team that week; however, as the sun inevitably rose on that fateful Saturday morning, he was no longer selected to play for the first team that week! This effective self-sacrifice to the club's hieratical slaughterhouse was initiated after Bill took a great personal vendetta to our then club captain, Ian, and his controversial assessment that to drop Carl Taylor to the second team would be of benefit to both team's chances of winning their respective league games. From memory, this conversation started at around 9pm on the Friday — it ended at 3am on the Saturday. Time was but a number in the course of our in-depth, mutinous like, conversations on the matter! Anyway, with the drinks flowing nicely and the verbal exchanges similarly, it was eventually concluded that yes; Ian was unequivocally wrong in his judgement to sideline Carl to the second XI that week. He had been making useful contributions to our 2016 campaign, not much worse than anyone else in the team; where consequently Billy took great umbrage at this! So much so, that at 3am, he composed an essay length text message as to Ian's grave error, and subsequently demoted himself so that Carl could play!

I eventually went to bed at 4am that morning; still unsure as to how this situation would resolve itself. I had a great three hours sleep until I was awoken to the sight and sound of booming laughter from Billy, Carl and Tom, who all had evidently just completed an all-nighter, or shall I say, 'saw the nets!'. But yes, it was revealed that Billy had followed through with his prior claim at 3am that he had indeed dropped himself in sacrifice for Carl!

So, with myself procuring three hours sleep; Carl with zero hours sleep; we ventured up to Ashford that Saturday morning to play Boughton and Eastwell CC. This is the little club that plays quite literally on the middle of a village green surrounded by a main road. Lovely, scenic ground; however, the look on Ian's face when Carl made a somewhat inevitable golden duck was nothing other than the 2nd best thing I had seen all year!

The Start

The Middle

The End

THE BATTING DEBACLE - 2016

As was the case that year, a team situated in the centre of Kent were our final opponents in the league before the curtain was drawn on the 2016 season, and to be frank, it was nearly my last. While writing this short memoir introduction, this cricket match brings forth such strong internal emotions where I was quite literally one inopportune comment away from completely giving up altogether on my participation of amateur village cricket. This was a game that made me feel like such an outsider in the sport that I have loved for so many years; and for those of you that do not know me, I show no emotion 99 percent of the time. This was the game that made me weep with uncontrollable sadness.

The away match started so well; a team photo was taken; everyone was in such high spirits that a middle of the league table finish had already been achieved! Consequently, we could all relish in the fact that beating the opposition would also send them plummeting down to the lower division! We won the toss and elected to field; and took up my usual position of crouching behind the trio of those all too familiar wooden poles for 40 overs. I obviously provided the usual 'chat' any keeper exhibits and thought, as usual, nothing untoward could occur following this. Granted, some jibes could have been a little blunt, but this is not unknown from my universally recognised demeanour. From memory, the opposition roughly accrued something within the region of a solid 220; give or take a few either side.

"*220!*" We thought.

"*Shouldn't be too difficult given it's a decent track!*"

As it happens, it wasn't, but the modus operandi in which we achieved their target is of such important note to me, that quite frankly, it must be tangibly written down due to the unparalleled significance it has had on my development of handling altercations with third parties.

After tea and again batting at five, I kindly offered my level one umpiring services to stand as the square leg umpire in the opening overs due to our unusual lack of providing one at the start of the game. This officiating endeavour didn't last too long, but boy, did I make an impression! To provide you with some context to justify my actions; personally as a keeper, I have been, on numerous occasions, 'no balled' when my gloves have encroached past the bowling crease while standing up to the stumps. Thus, whenever I get the honour of standing twenty-yards back on the leg side, I relish the challenge to reciprocate such facetious and meticulous umpiring on any unknowing, and probably less competent, wicketkeepers. The opposition's keeper on this occasion took great dislike at my umpiring philosophy, while also demonstrating an inordinate amount of umbrage at my rather particular and specific knowledge of this law of the game. Where, at the end of the over, after my blunt ruling, I attempted to explain to my wicketkeeping counterpart why his actions were penalised; to which his reaction, as well as many of the rivalling team's cohort, was of aggressive and abrupt in nature. Obviously, me being me, I elected that this reaction was not sufficient, and persisted on my ardent line of umpiring justifications.

Taking a retrospective view of these events, this was possibly the catalyst for why the future happenings occurred upon my arrival to the crease with the bat. Clearly, three wickets inevitably fell and I re-entered the figurative battleground! At this point in the story, the best way to describe the atmosphere on the field was not dissimilar to that of the tensions between Germany and Britain in September of 1939; one misplaced comment or action from myself, or the oppo, was quite frankly the cricketing translation of invading Poland! Predictably, this metaphoric invasion of our eastern European neighbours did occur in the form of an over celebration from their opening bowler, and the resulting send-off he provided which was aimed directly at my teammate, who also happened to be of Pakistani origin. I quote *"Thank god that shit is out!"* I didn't actually pick up on the implied jibe initially, but my replacement at square leg certainly did! They may not have intended for it to be derogative in context; however, given what had happened previously, it was certainly taken that way! Although my departing teammate did not hear this nauseating remark; possible racism is not something I could possibly subscribe to! Consequently, I couldn't possibly turn a blind eye to this implied Islamophobic behaviour! And evidently, I stood up for my Allah worshiping teammate; told them they were completely out of order, to which the reward for my bold actions resulted in a 'blitz' of abuse from the opposing eleven! As it happened, this was the literal tip of the very, very large iceberg!

Obviously, before any of their inferred slurs went past their hateful lips; I went about my batting as I always have; in my systematic and methodical way; checking of the guard at the start of every over and change of ends; the pushing down of the right pad, followed closely by the left, a tip of my trusty 2006 tour cap and ultimately ready myself to face the next ball. Now, after the dismissal of Kash; I'm now in a batting partnership with Harry Carter; Chris the chairman's youngest son. We were rotating the strike nicely at a semi-consistent rate, which to be honest, must have been a sweet metronomic delight to watch! The only way to describe the partnership would be that Harry and I scored a large amount of runs in an ever-repeatable routine; Harry scored one run – myself on strike – dot – I scored one run – Harry scored one run – myself back on strike; repeat routine. I could go on, but as you've probably guessed, this only increasingly infuriated them as each single was agitatedly taken. After many repetitions of this tedious and perpetual sequence of steady singles; the mid-Kent outfit were staring an inevitable defeat squarely in the face, and with it, their eventual demise in this league. Due to this, they concluded that I of all people was wasting time. Their summary to justify my perceived intentions could not have been anywhere further from the truth, and to be honest, I couldn't quite square the circle! One; I was innocently doing what my autistic brain compels me to do, and two; the light was fading quickly, so any aim of elongating the match would have only been in their favour! I was being called a 'See you next Tuesday' from here, there and everywhere! The loudest being from the long-on boundary! I also had the slip or keeper perpetually festering in my ear reiterating the same! Then, when Harry went on some 'Ben Stokes' or 'Jos Buttler' inspired counter-attack, things only went from bad to worse! From memory, he even cleared the 15-foot-high pavilion located on the midwicket boundary! So evidently, I couldn't withhold my great delight to this fact without obvious ambiguity. The reason for this dire gloating on my part, was that in 2016, Harry was only 13-years-old, so by him conducting these outrageous, pavilion-apex clearing acts off the bowling of fully-grown men; it would have almost been a disservice to Margate CC to not 'enthusiastically' congratulate Harry on his evidently explosive talent with the bat! This, to say the least, was like poking the hornet's nest; it enraged the 11 opposing players to the point that I think if I was not wearing the customary batting protection, and wielding a three-pound lump of willow, they might have elevated this phoney cricket war by introducing physical intervention to signify their anger at their mistaken perception of my 'obtrusive' batting technique and enthusiasm from the other end.

This apparent despise of me and my autistic battings traits, reached boiling point when I neglected to offer a shot that struck me high on my thigh pad and attempted to pinch a quick single. Competently, dead ball was signalled by the standing umpire, where I was instructed to return back to the striking end, and you guessed, upon my completion of my re-admittance to the popping crease. I had to once again, re-check leg-stump, push down my right pad, push down the left, tip the trusty 2006 tour cap, and ready myself to face the next ball. The bowler consequently provided me with the adjective that completed my metaphorical happy family of derogatory insults that day; where I was called a *"Fucking bell end"*. This was the final straw in my subjective policy of appeasement to their perception of me; I stormed down the other end and confronted this little fat bowler; called him as such, to which the umpire promptly positioned himself in between myself, and this appalling excuse for a human being to organise an impromptu minute silence on the middle of the square to calm this considerably heated affair. As cricketers, we all submitted to the umpire's demands and didn't utter a word for that time.

Furthermore, nothing more was said for the rest of the game. Clearly, we won the game; myself and Harry both scoring forty-odd; where we walked off the pitch thinking that this effective spirit of cricket holocaust had finally concluded. I thought that I could peacefully go into the bar, procure myself with a pint of water to rehydrate after my heroic innings, and enjoy the hour-long trip home listening to the timeless, smooth sounds of the likes of Frank Sinatra and Dean Martin et al,.

This ambition was nothing but a comprehensive delusion! Now, for those of you that don't know, altercations on the cricket field, 99 percent of the time, stay on the field. Odds were however against me that day and this happened to be the one percent! I entered the pavilion; politely asked for a pint of water and Craig a fruity cider. Where I was then greeted to the vilification in front of the entire population of the spectating patrons, by the same fielder from long-on whom had previously in the game, without an intermission for breath, bombarded me with that most delightful acronym of seeing me next Tuesday! He finished his public defamation of my character about how I had the audacity to even breathe the same air as him, let alone enter their newly refurbished clubhouse! He then proceeded to hold an ad-hoc referendum as to whether my presence in their precious new pavilion was even allowed! To which, unsurprisingly, he was the only advocate for my expedited removal of their newly-refurbished establishment.

Where comparatively, three months prior to these events in 2016, the UK's decision to leave the European Union was a close 52 percent; the decision taken upon this somewhat partisan home electorate, was one percent. This man clearly felt a sense of strong embarrassment to his poor electoral judgement. So, in something similar to David Cameron upon his loss, the long-on fielder promptly vacated the large room. Where I, probably unwisely, soon followed as I saw it appropriate, much like when umpiring earlier, to attempt to explain the situation behind these escalated events. Essentially, I tried to reason with the unreasonable; he wrongly assumed that if one is autistic, they do not know they are autistic. Unfortunately, although he is probably right in the case for a five-year-old child; I was 22 at the time and had gone through my entire life knowing I have always been 'slightly' different from my peers. Eventually, I concluded that this was a fruitless endeavour; he wasn't going to yield, and continually carried out what was effectively the oral variant of GBH. In front of my team and my own father, he said,

"You're a fucking disgrace! You should be ashamed!"

This was alongside some other supplementary adjectives that I won't elaborate heavily upon, but I suppose this did allow me to collect a second happy family that day, so I won in some respect!

Dad clearly heard this all, ordered me to sit in the car for my own physical safety, while he talked to the long-on fielder to support my prior explanation. He could see this man was readying himself to elevate the situation even further and wanted to help me. What happened after that, I don't know, I have never seen this man again; however, I was in an uncontrollable state of an unyielding surge of emotions that I had simply never felt in my life! While crying, which I don't often do, I was sat alone in the car, quite literally contemplating my continuation of playing cricket;

> "If this could happen once, it'll happen again, so should I even be playing for my own safety?"

Eventually, Dad cottoned on to how unreasonable this man was and gave up his own mediating efforts. Having been in that state for at least half the journey home, it was eventually concluded with Dad, that if this should ever happen again, I should remove myself from the situation entirely; retire hurt, admittedly emotionally, and return when tempers have calmed. I accepted this but also acknowledged that these events have fundamentally changed me while playing on the cricket field. Who even was I now? Could I even enjoy my Saturdays' in the summer moving forward? This, as I'm sure you get a feeling for while you read this detailed account of events, was another fork in my developmental road since turning twenty.

I did; however, continue playing, and thankfully this isn't the end of the book! I eventually also stopped picturing these events as I went to sleep some months later! However, I learnt that if sometimes one cannot reason with the unreasonable, one must accept this. But finally, and most importantly, I utilised this ruthless and severely unfortunate experience to build upon my underdeveloped social knowledge of the world; to try and protect myself from potential physical and mental harm in the future, on and off the cricket field. Yes, I still have a lot to learn. Yes, I still get in these disputes that need to be rectified by friends or family; often by Billy who wasn't there that day, but has done in the years since. But for any autistic person, whether they play cricket or not, they should take heed of this story and use the knowledge I learnt that day. A day, that I regard as one of the worst days of my life.

THE DAY I WAS BETTER THAN ZAK CRAWLEY (SORT OF!) - 2015 & 2016

The first Sunday in September of 2015 and 2016, the latter being the very next day after the batting debacle, are both days I will never forget for as long as I live! I participated in two games of cricket that even if one were writing it with the intention to be a work of fiction; it would be regarded as somewhat obscure and diametrically distant from any possible or believable truth. Simply put, anyone reading this could quite easily switch off entirely due to its implausibility! This tale however; happened in real life; in my life. To support this claim, there were many people witnessing; umpires; scorers, one of whom was my father; an entourage of tea girls and ladies; a spectating crowd; and even my own mother! These games are probably the closest that I, the Autistic Village Cricketer, will ever come to playing professional cricket!

From the title of the memoir and the introductory paragraph, you're probably thinking that I've got a lot to live up to; and you'd be right! So moving on, I was selected to play for the Hoppers Tie Club vs The Provender Select XI. Essentially, this was like playing in real-life games of EA Sports Cricket 07' because of who was playing in the matches! To provide you with some necessary context, these were games arranged in conjunction with a generous middle-aged man who owned his own cricket field in Faversham; hired a groundsman and invited eight teams a season to play his select XI. This ground was simply immaculate! I have never seen, let alone play at, such a picturesque cricket venue in my entire life!

Skippering the Hoppers side both years was none other than Matt Walker; ex-Kent top-order batsman and now the county's head coach! Over the two games, to quite obviously name drop for the benefit of this book, Zak Crawley, who has recently been selected for the England Test team played alongside me; as was the ex-Kent and England off-spinner James Tredwell; Matt Coles; Mitch Claydon and ex-Kent wicketkeeper and my godfather Steve Marsh, all playing in the same XI's as me; Josh Williamson; a 'Kent Regional 1A East Saturday League cricketer!'. Somewhat embarrassingly, I was nothing other than star struck! Where finally, to top off the star-studded list of names playing in the game; Martin Saggers was also drafted in to play for the opposition in 2016! Simply put, what a time I had in store!

In 2015, the Hoppers lost the toss and were invited to field. I cannot remember the scores of either game; however, I do remember the Hoppers ultimately winning both years. How we won though; your guess is about as good as mine. So, there I was, sharing the same field with over half the team consisting of a mixture of current and ex-professionals', all playing in the same game I have loved since a young boy! I was obviously trying to keep my cool; where probably, I was worrying more about how to interact with these life long familiar faces; all while attempting to hold my own on the pitch and not make a fool out of myself!

It didn't start too well; Matt placed me at backward point. Why? God knows! I couldn't help but think;

> *"FUCK! Over the course of the 40 overs, something would inevitably come my way and I would have to deal with it!"*

Was I right? Of course I was! It appeared the cricket Gods clearly bestowed upon me the title of 'ball magnet'. So, in something similar to my first-ever adult game all those years prior, and due to wicketkeeping exclusively for Margate, I let this ball that was travelling about as fast as a trickling snail through my ill-practised long barrier! Matt Walker must have been thinking that I'd never played cricket before! Fortunately, this misfield only allowed one run, so luckily, I wasn't moved by the ex-professional captain. I think though that surely one more mishap like that and it would have been curtains for any further involvement of fielding in an interesting position! But boy, what I produced next, was a piece of sheer, indisputable brilliance!

With a fair few overs now elapsed; James Tredwell was now bowling in conjunction with some other pro whose name currently eludes me, wherein utter shock to everyone watching, not to mention myself, I read this batsman's intention like a book! James was bowling to a left-handed Kent League division one opening batsman. With myself being one of the few amateur cricketers on the park, where this striker clearly witnessed my previous fielding mishap, it appeared he specifically targeted the general vicinity of me. So, with some considerable velocity, the opener produced this huge; extravagant; whooping reverse sweep manufactured explicitly to be hit towards me fielding at backward point! Clearly, in utilising my many, many years of playing experience, I foresaw this sneaky ploy well before connection was even made; taking one small, shuffle sized step to my right as he hit the ball; it rose sharply to shoulder height and just within an arms reach. Without even thinking about it, I put both my hands towards the general area of where I thought the ball was about to go. So with this ball now hurtling towards me; while not even looking at the ball; I — catch it! I bloody well CATCH IT! I was about as surprised as anyone! I instantly ran towards the middle and gave high fives to all my new professional playing peers, in something probably comparable to Monty Panesar! I did it!

How? It's quite frankly a miracle. But to this day, the situation behind said miracle, I now have the honour of telling virtually every new person I meet in the game. About how in a scorebook, somewhere, someplace, on this huge planet; it reads; bowled, Tredwell - caught, Williamson. Modesty is not even a factor when it comes to this great personal life highlight; it's like nothing other than a dream!

So, in 2016, after the fielding portion of that game was completed. Matt then asked me if I'd like to open the batting after a tea. Although I was somewhat apprehensive at first, due to my inside knowledge from the previous year that tea was comparable in size to a banquet made for Henry VIII, I accepted the invitation! To be honest, I would have been foolish to let an opportunity like that slip through my fingers! Admittedly, it would have also been a fairly poor show from this ex-fat man to hold back on the tea; however, opening the batting with a full stomach was categorically agreed! Batting with me was the then, Kent 2nd team opening batsman, and now capped England Test player; Zak Crawley. Obviously, at the time I didn't have a scooby doo as to who he was, or to become. For all I knew, he could have been a Gore Court Kent League batsman! Oh, how naïve I was! Looking back now, little did I know then, he would actually go on to make his First-class debut 11 months later vs the West Indies of all teams! So, with what I'm about to tell you, I did make myself look a bit silly!

Essentially, what transpired was that when we walked to the crease to commence the Hopper's innings, there was me, nothing more than just a humble village cricketer, in essence, trying to advise a future capped England Test opener; how to open the innings! I quote,

> "Alright Zak, take it easy. No need for any rash shots. Play yourself in and we'll rotate the strike, ok?"

Did Zak listen to me? No — no he did not. For the first ball of the innings, it looked like he might have taken on board my experienced and wise counsel, by producing my favourite, timeless and indispensable defensive cricket shot. The follow-up delivery, however; from memory was bowled on what looked like a 6th stump line; outside the off peg. Did Zak leave the ball? No. Did he play an extravagant extra cover drive? Of course not! Zak took a huge step across his stumps and fabricated something I've only ever seen in an international T20! He hit the ball that was originally so far outside his off stump, it would have probably been called a wide if he had left it! Then, as sweet as you like, he effortlessly lofted the ball over the midwicket fielder and scored a one-bounce four in the process! Needless to say, in a game that I've actually participated in; I've never quite seen anything like it!

Even though he evidently didn't give my sound advice the time of day; we actually made close to a fifty-opening partnership! How many I got in that substantial batting unison you ask? Six.

Out of 45 runs; I scored six of them! Let me just say that one more time for dramatic effect; I scored six runs out of a partnership of 45! To summarise the batting collaboration, I was, to say the least, 'slightly' outplayed in the variety of our shot selections. Having said that, it does take two to tango; I just happened to play the influential role of the attractive female dancer following the lead of her more dominate and talented partner! Clearly though, as I always do, I actually listened to my wise words; I played an attractive extra cover drive off the opening bowler that received a light applause from the somewhat inebriated crowd; I produced an eye-catching flick off the pads for two; but most importantly, I didn't play one rash shot. I did; however, play many – many renditions of the one shot I can safely say I executed with more conviction and effectiveness than Zak Crawley that day; the forward defence. Clearly, this is not intended in the slightest to be derogatory in nature, but just to reiterate and bring to the forefront; this a man who is now a capped England test player, and undoubtedly will open the batting for the national side many more times. So, in what is probably somewhat embarrassing for him; in a shot that should be his bread and butter as an opener, he was, in my opinion, categorically outperformed in this very, very specific domain of batsmanship by me, Josh Williamson; a Kent Regional 1A East Saturday League cricketer; who lives and breathes for the sport and pays for the privilege! Granted, in comparison to my unquantifiable number of dots in the scorebook (six off 26!); Zak only played one forward defence that day. However, the fact remains the same, and frankly readers, because of that, I can now die a happy and contented man! After all, he only scored one in his debut Test match innings! So perhaps he should have been taking notes!

This internal monologue of an unbelievable but completely true account of the events in 2015 and 2016 concludes with how I was finally dismissed. Two words spring to mind; Martin Saggers. Now, Mr Saggers has, I believe, a few test caps under his belt, and unsurprisingly, this next section centres around the ex-England bowler. Martin was, to say the least, ambling in to commence his spell; why? Perhaps he was being nice to me. The first ball he bowled; was a spot over pitched; on centre stump, and what did I do? Well, this village cricketer once again produced the unexpected; he drove one straight past his feet for an easy two. I thought,

> *"Shit! That probably hasn't helped my longevity at the crease now has it..."*

I was right, the next ball he fires down a delivery which must have been a good 10mph quicker than the previous warm-up; it was in line with my off stump, but it jagged away; luckily, it was too good for me to hit! Clearly, Martin had my number and he was about to ring it, I just didn't know when! Unfortunately for me, he knew exactly when to call me; it was the very next ball!

So, in the same scenario; it landed on the off stump, jagged away but slightly less than last time. It was as if he could physically control the seam movement off the pitch like the average joe can control swing; and moved it away just enough for me to gift a feather to the keeper. This dismissal was almost somewhat reminiscent of cricketers in yesteryear when they used to walk after nicking off. So, without even looking behind myself to check if the ball had been safely caught by the competent gloveman; I promptly tucked my bat under my arm; congratulated Martin on his apparent and efficient appraisal of how to dismiss me; and strolled off towards the white picket fenced pavilion, to enjoy some more of that free beer, and ever so delectable thickly-cut rare rib of beef!

Martin Saggers Getting me like a Kipper!

What a great time I had! Hopefully, in the future I can do it again! Isn't it strange though how the events in 2016, which is probably one of the greatest and most memorable days in my amateur cricketing career, can directly supersede possibly one of my worst. In life, I stand by the philosophy that all things happen for a reason, and this definitely is no exception to that rule.

Hoppers XI vs Provender XI 2015 Scorecard

Provender v Hoppers

Sunday, September 6 2015 at Provender CC

Hoppers Won By 85 runs

Provender won toss and decided to field

Hoppers	Provender
229 all out (34.3 overs)	144 all out (33.0 overs)

Hoppers

Batsman			Runs	Balls	4s	6s	S/r
M Claydon		b S Boyns	0	1	0	0	0.00
B Harminson	c S Boyns	b A Edwards	66	53	8	3	124.53
J Treadwell		b A Edwards	39	30	6	1	130.00
M Coles	c S Piesley	b A Edwards	23	13	1	3	176.92
M Hunn	c S Piesley	b A Edwards	11	12	2	0	91.67
S Marsh	c W Hilton	b A Edwards	18	21	2	1	85.71
S Miller	run out(N Sharp)		11	17	1	0	64.71
A Kent+		b N Sharp	4	17	0	0	23.53
J Williamson		b N Sharp	1	4	0	0	25.00
M Walker*	c A Campbell	b C Piesley	23	24	4	0	95.83
P Nicholls	not out		14	17	2	0	82.35
Extras	2nb 6w 2lb 9b 0pen		19				
Total			229 all out (34.3 overs)				

Batsman	Fall of Wicket	Partnership Batsmen		Over
M Claydon	1-0	0	M Claydon(0) B Harminson(0)	0.1
J Treadwell	2-86	86	J Treadwell(39) B Harminson(40)	11.2
M Coles	3-137	51	M Coles(23) B Harminson(26)	15.3
B Harminson	4-137	0	B Harminson(0) M Hunn(0)	15.5
M Hunn	5-151	14	M Hunn(11) S Marsh(2)	19.1
S Marsh	6-176	25	S Marsh(16) S Miller(5)	23.3
S Miller	7-184	8	S Miller(6) A Kent(2)	25.6
J Williamson	8-191	7	J Williamson(1) A Kent(2)	27.2
A Kent	9-192	1	A Kent(0) M Walker(1)	27.5
M Walker	10-229	37	M Walker(22) P Nicholls(14)	34.3

Bowler	O	M	R	W	Wd	Nb	S/r	Econ
S Boyns	5.0	1	38	1	1 (1)	0 (0)	31.00	7.60
J Eves	5.0	0	35	0	2 (2)	0 (0)	0.00	7.00
A Hussain	7.0	0	53	0	1 (1)	2 (2)	0.00	7.57
A Edwards	7.0	1	43	5	1 (1)	0 (0)	8.60	6.14
C Piesley	5.3	0	23	1	1 (1)	0 (0)	34.00	4.18
N Sharp	5.0	0	26	2	0 (0)	0 (0)	15.00	5.20

Provender

Batsman			Runs	Balls	4s	6s	S/r
S Plesley+	c J Williamson	b J Treadwell	38	60	3	2	63.33
C Marsh		b M Hunn	16	20	0	2	80.00
A Campbell		b B Harminson	2	12	0	0	16.67
W Hilton	st A Kent	b J Treadwell	24	23	5	0	104.35
R Cooper	c S Miller	b M Claydon	18	27	1	1	66.67
C Piesley	c A Kent	b M Coles	4	7	0	0	57.14
A Hussain	c and b	J Treadwell	3	8	0	0	37.50
J Eves	st A Kent	b J Williamson	12	28	1	0	42.86
N Sharp*	c P Nicholls	b M Claydon	3	10	0	0	30.00
A Edwards	not out		2	3	0	0	66.67
S Boyns	lbw	b J Williamson	0	1	0	0	0.00
Extras	1nb 20w 1lb 0b 0pen		22				
Total			144 all out (33.0 overs)				

Batsman	Fall of Wicket	Partnership Batsmen		Over
C Marsh	1-34	34	C Marsh(16) S Piesley(16)	7.6
A Campbell	2-46	12	A Campbell(2) S Piesley(10)	11.6
S Piesley	3-85	39	S Piesley(12) W Hilton(24)	18.4
W Hilton	4-92	7	W Hilton(0) R Cooper(4)	20.5
C Plesley	5-99	7	C Piesley(4) R Cooper(2)	23.2
A Hussain	6-102	3	A Hussain(3) R Cooper(0)	24.6
R Cooper	7-130	28	R Cooper(12) J Eves(7)	28.1
N Sharp	8-139	9	N Sharp(3) J Eves(4)	30.4
J Eves	9-144	5	J Eves(1) A Edwards(2)	32.7
S Boyns	10-144	0	S Boyns(0) A Edwards(0)	32.8

Bowler	O	M	R	W	Wd	Nb	S/r	Econ
M Walker	5.0	1	13	0	1 (1)	0 (0)	0.00	2.60
M Hunn	4.0	0	21	1	1 (1)	0 (0)	25.00	5.25
B Harminson	5.0	2	18	1	1 (1)	0 (0)	31.00	3.60
S Miller	4.0	0	27	0	2 (2)	0 (0)	0.00	6.75
J Treadwell	4.0	0	12	3	0 (0)	0 (0)	8.00	3.00
M Coles	4.0	0	17	1	5 (8)	0 (0)	29.00	4.25
M Claydon	3.0	0	6	2	0 (0)	1 (1)	9.50	2.00
S Marsh	1.0	0	19	0	3 (3)	0 (0)	0.00	19.00
P Nicholls	2.0	0	8	0	1 (2)	0 (0)	0.00	4.00
J Williamson	1.0	0	2	2	2 (2)	0 (0)	4.00	2.00

Match Report

Weather: Bright And Sunny Pitch: Drying

Umpires: Ken Amos & Barry Hulks

Scorers: Denise Short & Dave Williamson

Hoppers XI vs Provender XI 2016 Scorecard

Provender v Hoppers

Sunday, September 4 2016 at Provender CC

Hoppers Won By 2 wickets

Provender won toss and decided to bat

Provender	Hoppers
173 for 9 (33.2 overs)	174 for 8 (33.5 overs)

Provender

Batsman			Runs	Balls	4s	6s	S/r
P Geary	c C Piesley	b S Ruddock	45	72	8	0	62.50
R Cooper	c Z Crawley	b H Bernard	1	5	0	0	20.00
A Kent+	c S Nicholls	b C Hartley	11	22	0	1	50.00
A Campbell	c G Myers	b S Ruddock	24	25	3	0	96.00
J Waitt	c D Stevens	b C Piesley	11	11	1	0	100.00
O Oldroyd	c Z Crawley	b S Ruddock	6	2	0	1	300.00
T Palmer	c H Bernard	b P Nicholls	50	26	5	4	192.31
M Saggers	c P Nicholls	b C Piesley	7	11	1	0	63.64
J Eves	c M Walker	b D Stevens	9	19	0	0	47.37
S Boyns	not out		0	7	0	0	0.00
N Sharp*	not out		0	1	0	0	0.00
Extras	1nb 1w 0lb 7b 0pen		9				
Total	173 for 9 (33.2 overs)						

Batsman	Fall of Wicket	Partnership	Batsmen	Over
R Cooper	1-3	3	R Cooper(1) P Geary(2)	2.5
A Kent	2-33	30	A Kent(11) P Geary(15)	10.2
A Campbell	3-73	40	A Campbell(24) P Geary(14)	18.3
J Waitt	4-98	25	J Waitt(11) P Geary(14)	21.6
O Oldroyd	5-104	6	O Oldroyd(6) P Geary(0)	22.2
P Geary	6-105	1	P Geary(0) T Palmer(1)	22.6
M Saggers	7-142	37	M Saggers(7) T Palmer(30)	27.5
T Palmer	8-166	24	T Palmer(19) J Eves(3)	30.3
J Eves	9-173	7	J Eves(6) S Boyns(0)	33.1

Bowler	O	M	R	W	Wd	Nb	S/r	Econ
H Bernard	4.0	0	10	1	0 (0)	0 (0)	24.00	2.50
M Walker	4.0	1	10	0	0 (0)	0 (0)	0.00	2.50
C Hartley	4.0	1	12	1	0 (0)	0 (0)	24.00	3.00
Z Crawley	5.0	0	26	0	1 (1)	1 (1)	0.00	5.20
S Ruddock	4.0	0	33	3	0 (0)	0 (0)	8.00	8.25
C Piesley	6.0	0	26	2	0 (0)	0 (0)	18.00	4.33
P Nicholls	5.0	0	48	1	0 (0)	0 (0)	30.00	9.60
D Stevens	1.2	0	1	1	0 (0)	0 (0)	8.00	0.75

Hoppers

Batsman			Runs	Balls	4s	6s	S/r
Z Crawley	c R Cooper	b S Boyns	34	25	4	2	136.00
J Williamson	c A Kent	b M Saggers	6	26	0	0	23.08
G Myers		b N Sharp	17	33	2	0	51.52
S Ruddock	c A Campbell	b M Saggers	3	8	0	0	37.50
D Stevens	c and b	T Palmer	39	40	3	2	97.50
C Hartley	c A Kent	b M Saggers	1	4	0	0	25.00
C Piesley	not out		43	44	5	0	97.73
S Nicholls+	st A Kent	b M Saggers	17	19	2	0	89.47
M Walker*	c A Kent	b A Campbell	1	3	0	0	33.33
P Nicholls	not out		1	2	0	0	50.00
Extras	1nb 6w 1lb 4b 0pen		12				
Total	174 for 8 (33.5 overs)						

Batsman	Fall of Wicket	Partnership	Batsmen	Over
Z Crawley	1-45	45	Z Crawley(34) J Williamson(6)	6.6
J Williamson	2-52	7	J Williamson(0) G Myers(6)	10.4
S Ruddock	3-57	5	S Ruddock(3) G Myers(0)	12.1
G Myers	4-84	27	G Myers(11) D Stevens(15)	17.3
C Hartley	5-85	1	C Hartley(1) D Stevens(0)	18.3
D Stevens	6-129	44	D Stevens(24) C Piesley(20)	26.5
S Nicholls	7-171	42	S Nicholls(17) C Piesley(22)	32.6
M Walker	8-172	1	M Walker(1) C Piesley(0)	33.2

Bowler	O	M	R	W	Wd	Nb	S/r	Econ
S Boyns	5.0	0	18	1	0 (0)	0 (0)	30.00	3.60
J Eves	7.0	0	39	0	3 (3)	0 (0)	0.00	5.57
M Saggers	6.0	0	20	4	1 (2)	1 (1)	9.50	3.33
N Sharp	5.0	0	28	1	0 (0)	0 (0)	30.00	5.60
T Palmer	6.0	0	32	1	1 (1)	0 (0)	37.00	5.33
R Cooper	3.0	0	20	0	0 (0)	0 (0)	0.00	6.67
A Campbell	1.5	0	12	1	0 (0)	0 (0)	11.00	6.55

Match Report

Umpires: Keith Short & Barry Hulks

Scorers: Denise Short & Dave Williamson

LIVERPOOL IS AT HOME: THE PARABLE OF HOW I LOST MY VIRGINITY - 2016

With the 2016 cricket season nearing its conclusion, and my years left on this planet gradually decreasing as the Earth performs each rotation of the sun; I deemed it most appropriate that at the start of 2016 it would be a good idea to procure myself of a lady to finally put a firm stop to the cricket lads figuratively ripping me a new one, because I had not done so yet to a woman! To help meet that aim, in the run up to the end of the season; like any red-blooded 22-year-old would, I subsequently laid the solid and stable groundwork to fulfil, that somewhat superficial, and possibly misogynistic, life imperative of securing what was only supposed to be a 'winter girlfriend'. I consequently became 'good friends' with a lovely young lady, who in the least creepiest way, was only intended to be in my life during the off-season. Yes readers, I can confirm, what you are about to read is the story of how I, Josh Williamson, the Autistic Village Cricketer, lost my virginity. How on Earth does this have anything to do with cricket, I hear you ask? Well readers, all I can say is; all good things come to those that wait!

You won't have to wait long! To reiterate, this tale begins life in the middle of August 2016. So, after having met up several times with this girl, I consequently became well acquainted with her.

Whom for the benefit of this story, and to avoid any possible legal disputes with her; I shall substitute her real name with the pseudonym of 'Jamelia'. Now, Jamelia, to reiterate is not her real name, was a nice enough person, and was sufficiently pleasant to be in the company of. Why is her name 'Jamelia' for this tale though? Well, after the events of this memoir, as Billy thought there was resemblance, he issued her with the nickname of, 'Jimmy Hill'! Anyway, we obviously had some sort of connection; which was possibly orchestrated via my lifelong autistic ability to mask into a social crowd; however, a spark was noticeably there. Now, early on in this little mascaraed of a relationship, I promptly confessed to Jamelia the true circumstance that I was still a virgin at the age of 22, and only recently; as of April of that year in fact, had ever seen a vagina 1st hand, let alone participate in sexual relations with the opposite sex! She accepted this, although possibly not initially believing my true revelation at first, but as you will be eluded to later in this memoir, she did not doubt my somewhat embarrassing claim that I was currently in the midst of a 22-year famine of intimacy.

The Video Log!

Moving on, we swiftly arrive at the 27th of October; a few days after Jamelia's birthday. I inherently deduced that any woman of this sexual persuasion would love nothing more than to reap the virginity and innocence from their 22-year-old boyfriend. So, unbeknownst to her, I thought it would be the best thing since sliced bread to book a hotel situated in East Kent, and schedule a shopping trip for the next day. Where eventually, we would retire back at my home in Birchington to resume my personally envisaged sexual activities! This theoretical ideology; however, was unfortunately simply just that, a theoretical ideology...

It started so well! The hotel was booked; the car for the shopping arranged - the condoms bought. I for one was so excited about my perceived inevitable future, that I filmed a short video log for my best mates on one of the cricket club's group chats; probably overstating my innate anticipation around the said birthday activities, and that finally, finally, I would lose my virginity once and for all! So, Jamelia and I arrived in good time at the hotel to soak up the 'country' vibes of the establishment; enjoy some dinner and drink a little of my personally provided M&S Demi-sec Cava. I hoped this would allow things to mellow slightly for me, to somewhat calm my obvious and apparent nerves, and to fulfil my internal pledge that 2016 would be the year I end the ridicule.

Things were starting to get a little heated; juices were flowing; the blood was pumping. When she uttered the phrase that no man ever wants to hear, *"Not tonight Josh, I'm not ready".*

And so, for the first time in my autistic life; what I thought, compared to what I actually said were two entirely different; completely separate; polar apart entities! Even those three phrases quite simply do not describe what happened that night enough justice! What I thought was,

> *"I've put in all this work! How dare you bloody turn me down! You know I've never had sex before, and you knew I was nervous, so now, now of all times, you have royally fucked me over!"*

I obviously I didn't say this, so in a considerably higher pitch, what I said in practice was;

"No, no, no, no, noooo; that's absolutely fine, don't worry, you're ready when you're ready, just say when you are, and I will be too".

I then finished this comforting fabrication with that all too familiar phrase that apparently all girls adore;

"I love you".

She instantly cried; melted in my arms and hugged me as if to say she was sorry. I put up with this little act of endearment because friends and family have previously made me perfectly aware that this is the social convention amongst neurologically typical people; and thus, should be something to be cherished and enjoyed — I did not enjoy that hug...nor, have I ever enjoyed hugging people! To be quite frankly honest; I'm that firmly averse to it, I don't even enjoy hugging my own mother! I did however, like the sound of sexual intercourse. So instantaneously in that moment, I convinced myself that this would be the most efficient and proactive method to ascertaining the accuracy of my long-held deductions.

It then firmly struck me in the centre of my 22-year-old virginal face! This is probably the biggest dilemma of my young life! How on Earth could I explain this unravelled mess of events to my best mates!?!? I was the man hyping up my impending, long overdue, sexual success to my cricket friends not even 12 hours before! I clearly couldn't admit defeat to them; I had to say something and they would know if I lied; I'd only just successfully told a fib for the first time in my life to my new female friend; and here I was, about to say my second to my best mates! So there I was, lying on this bed in the small hotel room, in nothing but my boxers, trying to conjure up what on Earth I was going to tell my mates, as to why I didn't have sex for the first time in my life on the 27th of October. Then it suddenly dawned on me in the early hours of the morning! It was as if the Angel Gabriel appeared on the ceiling of that little bijoux hotel room and whispered into my sexually inexperienced ear exactly what to tell my cricket friends.

"She's on her period..."

...

"Bloody genius!" I thought. *"Nothing could stop me now!"*
So, wielding nothing but my phone for company to use in the lavatory; I messaged my mates exactly that; that Jamelia, for want of a less graphic word, was having a 'heavy' flow. The boys' couldn't believe my fictitious luck; clearly sending messages of consolement and shear solace that today, on the 27th of October, would not be my day.

The Message that started
it all!

As you can imagine, this little charade of implied intimacy continued for the next 48 hours; little touches here and there; the odd cuddle, you know the routine. Admittedly, the shopping trip was nice, but I still hadn't lost my virginity! Then that Saturday, I got a conveniently timed text message from Billy;

> "Josh, we are going to the Foresters pub tonight, there's a band on, are you coming?"

Evidently, my news year's resolution had not yet been fulfilled, so I promptly replied without even asking for her approval,

> "Yes I'm coming! Jamelia's coming too! What time?"

Clearly, Billy relished in this opportunity to embarrass one of his best mates; I just didn't know it yet! So, we got to the pub in good time; enjoyed a few drinks; couple games of pool; it was a nice start to the evening. With Billy thinking I couldn't have possibly lied about a woman's period obstructing my first sexual conquest; he then uttered this haunting phrase directed right at Jamelia,

"So, Liverpool's at home tonight then?"

It was a deathly silence from me, and muffled laughter from everyone else. It took multiple repetitions but eventually I cottoned on to exactly what he was eluding to; clearly Bill was providing a cryptic message for all those that were privy to my prior confession! Jamelia had no idea, as she thought I was being sincere in the room two days before; a period wasn't even on her mind; she just thought the Merseyside club were playing at Anfield! I obviously couldn't tell Billy that Liverpool wasn't actually at home; and so, quite literally, I was between a universally believed bloody rock. Yes, bloody rock! And an internal hard place! This quote was floated around for a good hour or two, where eventually Jamelia also cottoned on to what it actually meant; Bill might have even told her; I'm not entirely sure. However, she worked out what I had said to my cricket mates on the 27th and ran out the pub in floods of tears; clearly distraught! I obviously followed after her in an attempt to calm the situation and save this apparent open goal; evidently, I only elevated tensions between us! I thought,

"Nooooo! This is it! I will never have sex! Why am I so weird!?!"
Clearly, with nothing left in my mediating locker, I accepted my fate and went back in inside to confide in Bill. He subsequently assured me that he would sort the whole situation out and that all will be fine. Quite evidently, that metaphor for the Angel Gabriel was actually Lucifer in a very convincing disguise! The end was most definitely nigh...

What happened next is all a bit foggy. Jamelia was eventually calmed by Bill, and Dad picked us up at the usual time of 11pm. He was early on this occasion which probably only helped matters following the revelation. The date is now Sunday the 30th of October, 2016. It's 8am in the morning and I'm somewhat hungover, thinking this will be the last time that I will ever see the lovely Jamelia. Where, rather out of the blue and completely surprising to me in my bed at home; she requested my expedited discovery of a nearby condom in the top draw, and whispered the words that can never be forgotten. I quote - *"I'm ready"*. I obviously won't go into the graphic details of what actually happened, but it was penetrative sex! I had finally put my penis in a female's reproductive orifice! All I could think was;
"Yeeeees! One from one for Joshy! You hero!"
I later had a more elaborate thought that went something along the lines of;

"Well, everyone may as well call me Lazarus from now on, as literally no one, no one was expecting the rise of my genitalia that morning!"

Why she told me she was ready after the previous night's events; I still do not know to this day; I probably will never know. It was most likely down to the words of Bill after I retreated back inside. What was going through her head that morning after the Forresters Pub fiasco to consensually submit to my obvious end goal? Maybe someone else reading this can enlighten me?

Anyway, after that emphatic life-changing U-turn, I promptly put the date in my diary, so that every year I can reminisce upon these events. So that on the 30th of October year, after year, after year; after 22 years, five months and 18 days, I can celebrate what I like to call, 'Virginity Day'! As it happened, I yielded on my initial objective of a 2016/17 'winter girlfriend' and stayed with my first successful sexual conquest for two long, and looking back, probably laborious years. All I wanted to do was play cricket, but no. For two years, I experienced next to no runs; two years of playing one game a weekend, two years of foolishly abstaining from friendly Sunday cricket! But most importantly, it was two years of segregating my cricket friends and best mates! Eventually, and probably fortunately, this caused a large enough rift between her and my eternal true love that is cricket. Which readers, was the beginning of the end for me and Jamelia. She essentially provided me a non-verbal ultimatum; after all that time of intricately balancing cricket and her, I pretty much had to choose one or the other. Her; someone I initially consensually contracted to pleasure me for the first time, or cricket; the game I have loved since the age of nine, have played every weekend in the summer since, and quite frankly, get far more satisfaction and enjoyment out of than I do pretending to hug a human being! So, as if I was the umpire of my life; officiating the last over before stumps on day 4. The final ball of the penultimate day's play was bowled. With it pitching on leg stump, and hitting Jamelia squarely below the knee-roll in-front of middle! I had a decision to make. Was she out, or was she not out? After taking an extraordinarily long period of time to decide, the fielders were almost off the field; however, I decided to slowly raise that index finger. She was out! And that readers, is what I chose; I chose cricket! And if I'm being honest, it was the best decision of my life thus far, other than deciding to play the game in the first place! The fielders were shocked! They thought I had made my decision long ago! So, with quick haste, they subsequently rushed back to their positions and requested for the extra half an hour, where I emphatically agreed! The game, and day's play in the test match of life was not over! My cricketing journey would continue marching on! Which, if I'm being honest, I probably wouldn't even be writing this book now if I had declined that appeal. Undeniably, it wouldn't have been anything other than the umpire announcing,

"Over bowled, and stumps gentlemen".

Anyway, fast-forwarding slightly; while also providing you with a couple of spoilers for some future tales, 2019 has been the best year of my life to date! I was a free man; it facilitated comprehensive cricket World Cup watching; drinking after every Saturday game; even another stag-do to Cardiff and actually being able to play cricket to my hearts content! Life has never been so good! But finally, that decision to unshackle myself from my perceived female burden, has allowed me to explore life past solely one woman, and that is where I will finish this memoir; on one emphatic cliffhanger!

LIVERPOOL IS AT HOME: EPILOGUE

This all being said, I hope she had been happy in the years since; that she finds someone that doesn't forge a like for tactile human interaction like me, and enjoys long walks without a purpose. Clearly, we just didn't match, but I wish her every success in whatever endeavours she decides to peruse in the future. As I hope you would have realised from reading the majority of this memoir, I have tried to the best of my written abilities to retain her right to privacy, which I think is vital. As such, it should go without saying, that I do not mean any malice in documenting these events, as it ended rather amicably with her, we just didn't quite click. As the old adage goes - *'it was me, not her'*. But, not to recall this life changing circumstance, and to overlook look the significant happenings, which I'm sure is milestone for anyone, would not only be a disservice to this literary publication, but it would also be doing my ageing self a considerable injustice to let the memory of how I lost my virginity fade with the sands of time.

TALK OF THE TOWN! - 2017

This next tale is not situated in a summer season of any year spanning between 2003 and 2019, it is; however, the only notable game of indoor cricket that is worth the time and effort to even consider penning an additional section on. This game comes in the form of a division one fixture, or shall I more accurately say; 'slaughter' vs our close geographical good friends at Broadstairs cricket club. To begin to paint you a picture of the circumstance surrounding said game, although it does sound great that in principle the nationally renowned Margate cricket club were playing in the top tier of the local indoor cricket league; and hence should be something that is universally celebrated. In practice, our membership of that particular division was comparable to Jesus being crucified on the cross; a slow and very painful death! To provide you with a little extra context, we hadn't won a game in division one for three long years. The league wouldn't even relegate us! It was quite literally like Hotel California; we could check out any time we wanted, but could never leave! So, with Broadstairs holding the crown of the best team in the league, even defending a hundred runs would have been enough for this league ruling outfit! Hence when they scored 213 against us, it was essentially like kicking a dead puppy; we were never going to move from our lifeless position! This game against Broadstairs in the winter of 2017, was quite frankly, nothing other than the figurative representation of the Roman executioners residing over our crucifixion and decided that enough was enough! Concluding that even Margate cricket club does not deserve this anguishing torture any longer!

For those of you that are unfamiliar with the rules and regulations of indoor cricket; essentially, the game is over and done within an hour; 12 overs each side, and just like in outdoor cricket, the winner of the game is the team that scores the most runs! On this occasion, I think we may have 'forgotten' that most important and essential imperative of winning a game of cricket! I won't go into how they accrued this many runs, but when batting first, Broadstairs scored 213. Yes! 213 runs in 12 overs! From memory, I believe Harry Brooks got physically clobbered for 81 runs in his three overs! To highlight this scenario even further, in theory the maximum all one can go for is 36 in an over; so you can do the maths! I think our calculated 'forgetting' of how to win a game of cricket could be forgiven on this occasion! This will; however, be explored in due course as the league didn't quite agree with that sentiment.

So, utilising our prior knowledge of playing this formidable team when we scored a nosebleed educing 42 vs their 150 in the previous game of the 2017 indoor season. We as a team unanimously voted that attempting to match their double ton-plus score would be a worthless, and futile exercise to even consider chasing. I also actually think it was a division one record if I'm being brutally honest! This being said, it was decided that to bat the 12 overs out, losing no wickets in the process, would be the most effective way to metaphorically display the back of one's middle and index fingers to the bulling Broadstairs CC and the league administration for their lacking cooperation in relegating us! We were subsequently instructed that to even attempt running between the wickets or trying to score boundaries, would be penalised with Brett's deathly glare! So, it was agreed by the whole team that the two best men for this rebelling mission would obviously be myself. After all, I had a better forward defence than Zak Crawley the year before, and Harry Brooks; another competent player who plays the shot well. Not as well as me, but acceptably proficient.

With myself preparing to bat, knowing full well this was going to bore the living daylights out of Broadstairs for the next half hour; Harry and I punched gloves; gave each other a reassuring nod; and started the task set upon us! With myself taking strike for the first ball, I was a bit nervous; the whole weight of the team was on my shoulders! I couldn't let them down! Did we get out? Of course we didn't! As it happened, Harry and I produced performances comparable to Monty Panesar and Jimmy Anderson in the 2009 Ashes! Nothing could even get remotely past us! There was almost an umbrella field from the four Broadstairs fielders; a slip, someone close enough to constitute fielding at short leg; a silly point and silly mid-on; they had it all! But they still couldn't get us out! We were hearing all sorts of distasteful and derogatory remarks from the spectating crowd in the viewing gallery above;

"What even is this?!"

"This isn't cricket!"

"How dare Margate play this way!"

"They should be banned from the league!".

We quite literally heard it all! But this only spurred on the defensive duo to complete the innings and carry our bats! All Harry and I could do was, and to quote the DreamWorks moving picture Madagascar, *"Smile and wave boys', smile and wave..."*

It was utterly fantastic! Harry and I were successful in our pre-set mission proposed by Brett and seconded by everyone else! This achievement was made even greater by Margate being the only topic of conversation in the local cricket community for at least a fortnight! I even heard it on the grapevine that one of the umpires threatened to abolish us from league. He charged us with not playing the game in the right 'spirit' as were shaking hands. Our witty reply at the end of the game was with a simple, one-line justification to defend our apparent lack of trying;

> "Taking wickets in cricket is just as important than scoring runs".

No reply whatsoever could be thought of to our figurative mic drop! It was completely sound in both principle and practice. The umpire clearly wanted to make an example of us but was blatantly incapacitated in his efforts!

NAN'S LAST KNIT - 2018 & 2019

This next memoir is a heart aching and genuinely moving tale about how my Nan, who sadly passed away in April of 2019, after a short battle with cancer; fulfilled her pledge to replace my lost cricket jumper and completed her final quest in her long life to finish her last ever knitting project.

This tale begins in April of 2018; a year before my nan's death. We were playing away to Willesborough CC in our first fixture of that season. At the time, I had a sleeveless woollen acrylic jumper, which I absolutely loved playing in! One thing led to another that fateful day and for whatever reason, I forgot to put my, then, favourite jumper in my bag at the end of the game. Consequently, I have never seen it again! Seeing that Willesborough were over an hour away from my home in Birchington, driving there to retrieve, must like my lost hat in 2012, was logistically not an option on account of petrol and time. With myself clearly upset, the next day I told Nan about how I lost this jumper, where she, in her loving maternal way, said this sentence that I will take to my grave;

> *"Don't worry Josh, I knew you loved playing in that jumper, so I will make you a new one; it will take some time, but I will finish it!"*

This was nothing short of amazing. Nan was always eager to make me a cricket jumper since I was a little boy, but I wouldn't let her on account that wool is itchy on my skin, so now was the perfect time! In hindsight, looking back at it now, it could have actually been the catalyst for what was sadly in our immediate future.

Moving swiftly on to Christmas of 2018; Nan's cancer was starting to take a firm hold on her health. Although she could attend the annual after lunch boxing day gathering at our house; she couldn't make the usual lunch. This noticeably made Grandad visibly upset, so much so, that this was the first time I had ever seen tears start to swell from his eyes. Nevertheless, we enjoyed the get together after the meal, and Nan looked like she did too, although evidently in pain whenever she moved. Why I bring this up now is because I think it was the first realisation in Grandad's mind that he knew this would be his wife's last Christmas.

But Nan carried on fighting! She hadn't given up on her pledge that she made in the April of 2018! She valiantly fought every idea of giving up due to her ill-health, and ultimately won this last battle of willpower and motivation, before losing the mortal war to humanity's greatest foe; cancer. In the March of 2019, myself, Grandad, Dad, my two brothers', one of my uncles' and Nan sat around the TV at their home to watch England play Italy in the Six Nations. This was the day that Nan finally gave me her finished article! It fit like a glove! It was absolutely perfect, and I couldn't wait to play in it! I just hoped Nan would still be about to see a video of me doing just that! That was one of the first, and only times I've ever hugged my nan in my 24 years on this planet; she knew I hated touching and affection; but for her, for that amazing gift; I looked past that and gave her a hug that day. I couldn't see her face, but I like to think that it made her day and probably even her year! Unfortunately, she didn't make it to the day I first played in it; and having said that, it was coincidently played at Willesborough where I lost my original jumper a year prior! Although she wasn't alive then, I still like to think she saw that moment.

Nan's Jumper: Wearing Nan's Jumper the First Time I Took the Field (20/4/19)

On the 14th of April, Nan died almost exactly to the day a year after she so enthusiastically said she would make me a new jumper. With myself clearly distraught about my nan's death, her funeral was in May of 2019; a few days before my 25th birthday. It was a great send-off for the old gal! Many moving tributes, speeches and conversations were held to celebrate her life! This included my speech at the service, in front of the congregation at the church; it was a poem; a poem for my nan. And it read:-

"Nan, this was your last knit.
Let's just hope the runs come quick.
Even though you're no longer here.
I'll still play cover drives with no fear.
The jumper you've made, I will wear with pride.
So when I take the field, you'll be by my side."

There wasn't a dry eye in the house at Nan's funeral on the 9th of May, and my poem only worsened the collective mourning! It just so happened that my first league game in 2019 was on the 11th; two days after. It was so fitting that on that day, I played a classic 'Josh' innings on my way to making fifty-odd, when we were three or four down for not many. I have eternally attributed that innings to Nan, even though we lost.

I digress, little did I know, at the funeral, Grandad also confessed to me that Nan didn't actually make the jumper once; she even didn't make it twice; she made it three times because she was unhappy with the look and fit of it. That to me is a great testament to Nan's perfectionist attitude and that if something is worth doing, it must be done right! Because of the circumstance around the jumper, to this day, I have to triple check in my bag at the end of every game to make sure I have not repeated the forgetful actions from April 2018, that instigated the creation of this thing in the first place! If I were to lose that eternally sentimental jumper; knowing full well it was the last thing my nan ever made; I would never, ever, ever forgive myself.

I think, by taking a somewhat philosophical perspective on the event; this is the quintessential reason why I think all things happen for a reason. To reiterate, I am not a religious, or even a spiritual man; but I wholeheartedly believe that to be the complete, unadulterated truth! If I hadn't of lost the original jumper a year before in 2018; Nan would have never made of me her new one. And that, by also possibly floating around some conjecture, could have been one of the reasons why she held on for as long as she did in the early months of 2019. I don't know, but possibly, finishing that jumper was her reason for living when death was loudly calling her name.

Julie Williamson 19th July 1939 - 14th April 2019

CARDIFF… NOT AGAIN! WHAT COULD POSSIBLY GO WRONG!?!? - 2019

Yes! You have read the title of this tale correctly! Three years after our first visit to Cardiff for Brett's stag, we returned; but this time with something to prove! At the beginning of April in 2019; myself, Brett, Dan and Billy all made the journey back to the personal character-forming city to experience the capital of Wales one - more - time. The reason for this second visit, I hear you ask? Unbelievably, it was for Billy Woollard's stag! Yes, readers! Billy was getting married! We were all thinking it; how on Earth has this man who chatted up girls in the corner of the room while I was dead; the man of the consecutive cricket week shaggings'; the man who tried to stick his finger up Posh Bird's bum; and finally, how is the man who fell in love with Beth the stripper; getting married!?! Well, two words is the answer to that; Danielle Witherington. After a night the previous year where Bill had a drunken argument with his nan, he ordered Danielle to get a taxi back to his and wait for him until he got back. Bill was hours late as he wouldn't leave me until Brett arrived, where he popped the question as the clock struck 2am; she said yes! After years of knowing each other at work in a Ross and Rachel style, 'will they, won't they' relationship; where Danielle even turned Bill down by saying that she'd *"Rather shit in her hands and clap!"* Where after a few months of Billy's persistence, they finally got together and Billy popped the question!

Clearly, we made it in one piece to Cardiff to begin round two; three nights of pure mayhem were planned! Dan suggested that from his comprehensive experiences while at University, a 'shit shirt' night was a good idea and something we should do as a group. Now, for those of you that are not familiar with a shit shirt night, essentially it is an evening where a group of people wear the worst looking shirt possible. Why? Because at the time, half of this group were single, and apparently it provides an effective starting stimulus for conversing with the opposite sex! Obviously, as a relatively newly unshackled male, this sparked my full and enthusiastic attention! As such, before leaving, we all purchased a shirt that wasn't very pleasing to the eye.

As we had such a good time in Live Lounge in 2016, this evidently was the first place on the agenda for Bill's small stag party. So, with all four of us wearing our newly purchased shit shirts and a somewhat different air of confidence surrounding us, we made haste to our, then, favourite drinking establishment in Wales. This, however, was not before that evening's Europa League affair in which Dan and Brett insisted that we watch! Evidently, with myself clearly not interested in this 2nd tier of European football clash, I, to the conscientious worry of their doormen, elected to have a little doze in the middle of this sizeable pub to recoup my energies for later that night. Along with consuming my second burger of the evening, after having my first in the nearby Harvester!

So, with the football now finished, it was finally time to go to Live Lounge! Finding it, however, was for some reason problematic! So, when we eventually reached our holy grail of live music and cheap drinks, I loudly bellowed the crude phrase,

"We're here mother fuckers!!"

Now, as anyone that knows me, I am not exactly the 'quietest' of personalities. So, when I say, 'loudly bellowed', I really mean, shouting to such a volume that my mother and father could have undoubtedly heard me from virtually the width of Britain away in Birchington! This was subsequently, and probably unsurprisingly, also heard by the doormen at Live Lounge who proceeded to come to the rational deduction that this

ineloquent announcement came from Billy, not me! Consequently, due to their perception that he was too drunk to enter, this meant that they would not let him into to the much hyped-up bar, and we were sent the other way to allow him to 'sober' up! Now, if I'm being honest, Billy was, for lack of a better

Woken up in the Large Pub

word, the least inebriated out of all four of us! Clearly, he obviously must naturally 'ooze' the persona of a raging alcoholic! As a result, we ambled towards McDonald's so Bill could waft down three - 99p cheeseburgers; finishing the last outside the pub in view of the bouncers. He did actually buy four burgers that evening but one of which found its way down my gullet unsurprisingly! Needless to say, keeping up with traditions of 2016, this was my third of the evening! Anyway, this little charade appeared to appease the Live Lounge heavies — for now.

With the doorman now seemly off our coattails, we naïvely thought we could finally enjoy the bar in which we had perpetually discussed at periodic intervals for three years! We thought wrong. The bouncers were not off our coattails; they effectively soldered themselves to them! It wasn't long before our party of four became a party of two; those two consisting of Dan and myself. The two people who were most under the influence of alcohol, were the last two standing! This, however, was not before I did a rather large and sizeable 'boo-boo'. With Billy and Brett almost acting like my chaperones before their untimely forced exit; I proceeded to utilise my newly maintained, devilishly handsome good looks to take full advantage of the pre-planned shit shirt night. I just happened to emphatically bark up the completely wrong tree! Now, to ensure this tale is not as long as the book 'War and Peace'; from what must have looked like from any passerby, I was scouting, or shall I say 'hunting', the dance floor for any willing participant who possessed a nice smile and genitalia of the female variety. Now, while I was 'doing the rounds' of the dance floor, not unlike a shark circling his prey, this, not unattractive blonde woman fulfilled this succinct and somewhat simplistic criteria. However, unbeknownst to me this not unattractive woman had a boyfriend! I did notice her male friend; I just simply concluded that he was about as gay as a unicorn in the centre of Brighton, and thus caused no competition for this 24-year-old. As it happened, he apparently wasn't gay. He was actually her partner! And as you can probably guess, with my ability to interpret social cues already biologically impaired, he didn't like it when I then imposed myself on his, not unattractive girlfriend! One thing let to another, but clearly, this little altercation didn't end too well for me! Where outside, it would not be an understatement to say, it escalated in a rather expedited fashion! Resulting in Billy throwing his pebble sized iPhone right into the middle of the closeted boyfriend's forehead; almost returning from whence it came! It was all a little too much for me, so I retreated back inside, leaving Bill with nothing but a broken phone and a slow walk to a taxi with Brett! Clearly my great escape into the confines of Live Lounge, only left the hawk-like bouncers to re-focus their unrelenting gaze at mine and Dan's shit blue and yellow shirts! Which from there, I have absolutely no idea what happened, apart from learning a new life lesson!

The Shit Shirts!!

HOW DIDN'T WE FIND THIS PLACE BEFORE?!? - 2019

After the little bust up the previous night, the next night we stumbled across a bar that we didn't know even existed in 2016; Coyote Ugly! Little did I know, this place where we turned down an offer the previous night to go to the Live Lounge, was a chain of bars based off the film of the same name. If you haven't seen the film, which I hadn't at that point, is a place where girls, wearing very short shorts dance on the bar where one also purchases their drinks. This place is nothing other than heaven on Earth! It was so good, the remaining two nights we went there and nowhere else.

This place had it all! Clearly, the dancing girls were the main attraction; however, there was a mechanical bull in which one had to sign a waiver to ride; absolving the establishment; a posy of Oompa Lumpas' to keep us company; a kebab shop adjacent that served chip shop chips; YES! Chip shop chips! It had it all! This is also not mentioning the Gypsies that lingered around the smoking area to flog their quite evidently hyper-inflated tat. To discuss this strong traveller presence outside this almost make-believe establishment; this scruffy old lady, not dissimilar to the crazy cat lady in the Simpsons, proceeded to gain my unknowing attention to try and sell me a pair of flip flops for five whole pounds. Now, this pair of summer footwear was obviously bought from Poundland, where I subsequently called here out her on her 500 percent markup and declined to buy them! Apparently, she then tried to gift me some little trinket because I publicly outed her on her poor business model! To which I then began to take the memento from her ageing hand; where Billy slapped my hand out the way and justified his abrupt behaviour to the reasoning that it was a curse! Having said that, looking back, I was silly to even consider accepting her enchanted present. Where to calm the raised situation, Bill elected to haggle with the figurative crazy cat lady, by negotiating the purchase of her flip flops the following night for a lower price of £4.50! After all, he didn't want to be cursed as well!

Sensing unease, we vacated Coyote Ugly to go back to one more place on our nostalgic trip of Cardiff's nightlife; The Pleasure Palace. Now this trip wasn't as eventual as last time, Bill didn't particularly want to go, but Dan and I were very insistent upon our revisit! This time however, it was Dan doing the falling in love in the Pleasure Palace; who was she? God knows. However, I will leave this section with one last sentence. Bill must have spent at least £150 last time in 2016; Dan; over £300. His face was a picture when he saw his bank account the next morning; it was as if he had lost his house!

Hungover? Or Has Dan Just Seen His Bank Account?

The World Cup Final - 2019

It's Sunday the 14th of July, 2019; England were playing New Zealand in the Cricket World Cup final! What a day! Simply amazing! It is probably the case that these words will not do the day justice; however, penning the events I must! As you are aware, in the lead up to the final there were seven weeks of non-stop cricket, where I had the privilege of viewing every game involving every team, due to my Masters thesis being practically finished by the start of the tournament. The semi final vs Australia, which was played the Thursday prior, was already a messy day with the ad-hoc agreement to watch it at Bill's. The people present for the semi were Bill who was off work as he had just come back from his holiday in Turkey, Carl who was 'on-call', and me, essentially having a gap year in-between writing a 26 thousand word thesis, and hence my attendance was a given! Obviously, it doesn't need writing that England won that game with ease, and as such set up a Margate CC collective viewing with a BBQ on the Sunday at Billy's nan's!

Before the start of the game, after collecting Carl from his home, we had to make a necessary supply drop at Tesco. Me being me, I wrapped an England flag around my neck and was the pain in every shopper's bottom who had the audacity to not be

The Outside Seating

preparing to watch the game that day. Shouting at the top of my lungs *"It's coming home!"* Yes, I got some dodgy looks, but it was the biggest day in English cricket since the 2005 Ashes! Nonetheless, the cricket gods looked favourably upon the English that day in more than one sense; the weather was scorching! As a result, Carl brought around his four-meter HDMI cable to Bill's nan's so we could take the TV outside and watch the game under the blazing sun! With the supplies now gathered, we started drinking at 11am that day and it certainly showed by the end! So, with the food cooking by Danielle and Tom's other half; beer and wine flowing a little too freely, and myself accumulating an 'attractive' new tan line, the day was undoubtedly set up for a grand finale!

The time was 7.26pm; I'm shovelling bread down my gullet in a poor attempt to sober up and remember this moment where Jofra Archer commenced his run up to bowl the fifth ball in the super over. With England needing to defend three off two balls a yorker is bowled! One run scored with New Zealand needing two to win as England scored more boundaries in the game. It's now 7.28pm and there were four very, very drunk amateur cricketers with a heartbeat of 150 beats per minute in attendance; Jofra runs in one final time and Guptill could only tap the ball to Jason Roy at midwicket! They run the first without issue, but upon Roy's sufficiently accurate throw to Buttler it was good enough to allow him to dive and destroy the stumps; bringing forth a historic and emphatic World Cup victory! Billy's nan's garden erupted with a surge of noise comparable to that actually at Lord's! Chairs went flying, cider cans thrown with true disdain; and I, most uncharacteristically, even gave Carl Taylor a hug, that if I'm being honest, went on for a little too long it got a bit creepy! But it didn't matter; England had won the World Cup! If someone had said to me at the start of the summer as to my preference of England winning the World Cup or winning the proceeding Ashes series; the World Cup would have been instantaneously chosen! Oh, what a day!

That Hug... Sorry Carl!

At the semi final I made the bold declaration that if England won the final, we would open a bottle of Mote champagne to celebrate; we opened it and it was off! But that didn't matter, it was the sentiment implied that was the most important factor!

The game was; however, only the tip of the iceberg; McDonald's was ordered, the game highlights watched at least four times; and a 3am bedtime issued!

It was days after when I was again the subject of discussion in the Woollard household. The great mystery of who broke Bill's nan's light in her garden? Evidently, after throwing the garden chair, Bill clearly blamed me in this World Cup version of Cluedo; however, it was some weeks later that it was discovered the chair didn't even touch the light due to the supporting video graphic evidence. It was simply a faulty fixing in the light; possibly caused by the eruption of four inebriated and enthusiastic supporters!

The Off-Champagne for the Winners!

The Chair Throwing!

I'm Not Even Sure Why This Picture is Here!

LORD'S WITH THE LADS! - 2019

Later that month after the momentous World Cup victory; England played Ireland in a one-off Test match at Lord's. Upon Carl's discovery that the tickets for the game were only £25 each; Brett, Billy, Myself and Carl jumped at the chance to see yet more history be created in this summer to end all summers! In the run up to day three of the game. The day we were due to go, England, to put it bluntly, had the worst of starts to their 2019 test campaign. They were bowled out for 85 in their first innings; where additionally Ireland were pretty much cleared up after day one. So, we were not sure as to whether the game would even last three days; however it did, just about...

On the morning of the game, Brett had to bail as his son wasn't very well but kindly offered to drive Carl and myself up to the 02 Arena to make our transit to the game as easy as possible. I say 'Carl and myself' and not Billy, as Billy elected to join his old club for a game in their cricket week the previous day. Needless to say, he was a state when he found us at the tube station! Billy joined Carl and me, having not washed; only slept about four hours; and still drunk! To make matters worse, he was required to jump over the Old Wilsons wall to get to his parked van in their premises; which resulted in him having to buy an entirely new outfit from Primark because the clothes he was going to wear were covered and completely ruined by the wall's anti-climb paint! Needless to say, the day started as it went on!

With Billy just about successful in his mission to meet myself and Carl on time to watch the first ball of day three at Lord's; we eventually found ourselves waiting at the home of cricket's gates. It was here where I started to show the typical signs of someone with my condition; it was busy and we were packed liked sardines to enable our entry into the ground. I was quite literally sweating like a pig in an abattoir! Bill saw this so he reminded me that I do have an ASD card for situations just like this, and suggested that I show it to a guard and gain entry via a side gate.

> *"Great!"* I thought. *"I won't have to wait in this crowded line much longer!"*

Having said that, although our unenviable state of 'fish in a tin' wasn't helpful, the excess quantity of perspiration omitting from my hairy armpits probably wasn't helped by the addition of a smuggled bottle of red wine in my bag! Now, for those of you that don't know. Lord's is the only professional ground in the world where for international cricket fixtures, they allow one bottle of wine to be carried into the ground for personal consumption. With us clearly intending to be there all day, one bottle of wine would simply not be enough to last the duration! I needed extra supplies!

Knowing full well an eagle-eyed Lord's steward would inspect every nook and cranny of my rucksack before allowing us to even walk into the sacred ground; the day before I had preempted this eventuality.

"What did I do? I hear you ask.

"How did you hide the bottle?"

Well, in the lead up to our trip to the capital, by deciding to hide this bottle of red wine, I didn't just mask this thing with a jumper or something more ordinary! Oh no! It was intricately packed within a hollowed-out French stick, pretending to be my lunch! It didn't quite fit around the entire bottle though. So, in a genius display of creativity, my mother then conjured up the idea to wrap the wider bottom half in a thick layer of tin foil. Where in 'garnishing' this liquid luncheon disguise, she then dressed the top with the most limpest bit of wet lettuce she could find! To be honest, what she orchestrated that day could have even fooled the Enigma machine! Anyway, I think this was why I was panicking so much, as essentially I was like the wine variant of a Pablo Escobar drug maul!

The preliminary ticket checker of course allowed me to walk through the side gate, where I soon found myself in front of the bag checker. After I hauled the overly-heavy rucksack over my shoulder and unintentionally slammed it onto the trestle table, it made this most noticeable 'tink' sound. I thought to myself;

"Oh God! You must have heard that! If you ask one question it will be curtains for us watching any cricket today!"

I say 'curtains', as anyone who is aware of the difficulties people with autism can face, they tend to be terrible at lying! Any question, innocent or likewise, would have meant giving the game away and that guilty 'tink' probably just sealed my fate! So, there I was, slowly opening the zip in the optimistic hope that he didn't care, and would simply wave me though to my seat in the stands. After taking an inordinately long time to reveal the contents, the guard grabbed his torch and didn't utter a word as he started digging for any fermented contraband! With the sweat now dripping off my youthful brow, he looked in the left corner; nothing. He glanced towards the right; he looked towards the right again! Where he instantly darted his attention up towards my ever-increasingly worried self!

"Shit!" I thought. *"He knows! I'm probably going to get banned from Lord's for life!"*

The guard subsequently inhaled a large gulp of air to signify he was about to say something where he — let me through to enjoy the cricket! How? I will never know! But I was free and would not get banned from the home of cricket! My neurotic ASD concerns were wrong!

Anyway, after that little pickle of actually getting into Lord's and just about negotiating safe passage with my smuggled contraband, it was now time to enjoy some cricket, some conversation and, as it happened, also some gone off wine! The cricket was good, although short; England bowled Ireland out for thirty-something and won within an hour! The chat was great! Safe consumption of the wine;  however, not so much. After a gin and tonic and one glass of wine, I somehow managed to spill a spec of red wine on my perfectly white cotton shirt collar. Bill unsurprisingly informed me of this fact, to which I evidently attempted to rub the mark off; making it noticeably much, much worse! To make matters even fraught, having sunk a bottle and a half by this point and wondering the perimeter of Lord's with a half-full glass; this rather attractive twenty-something blonde girl nudged past me, which resulted in the entire bottom corner of my expensive white shirt look like I was caught short while on my menstrual cycle! There was only one way to temporary rectify the situation; tuck it in and look like some twat from the Oxford Bullingdon Club!

So, the cricket had finished and time on our visit to Lord's was over, and hence we were required to make haste back home. After a fair few more pints in the pub near the train station. Upon trying to obtain a receipt for my wrongly bought train ticket, I somehow got lost in the station! I had Bill on the phone chasing after me around the station for what must have been a good ten minutes; and me in floods of tears running down my face as I was running around this place like a headless chicken! I thought I was never going to get home! I must have looked like a right prat with my newly bought floppy hat from the Lord's shop and a tucked-in, wine-soaked shirt; missing my train home! Anyway, we did manage it home and it's now all in the past, however I will leave you with this little tidbit. I finished this day exactly how Billy started it — like a drunk, broken man, who needed new clothes...

ALMOST SAVED THE DAY PART 2 - 2019

This next tale is situated again in July of 2019; one week after the World Cup final. Following the chaotic scenes at Lord's the previous Sunday, it appeared that clearly all 22 players participating in the subsequent Saturday league game craved a little slice of the nail-biting action! To describe how I personally fit into this action-packed memoir; we were playing away to Canterbury, where they achieved a below par score for Polo Farm of 182. This was probably due to the soft, 'pudding' like texture to the pitch, where we fortunately won the toss and inserted them into bat! Needless to say, due to the low bounce of the pitch it was essentially compulsory for me to stand up for 39 of the 40 overs; conceding only one bye and snatching two sharp stumpings' in the process! Although I did drop one off Carl Taylor's bowling, where the opener happened to go on to make seventy-odd!

Anyway, with the game nicely poised at tea and Canterbury setting us a very gettable 182; our reply started so well! Both our openers; Carl and Mike, seeing us to 80-0 at drinks. We thought with only 103 to win off 20 overs with all our wickets remaining, it should be a very leisurely stroll in the metaphorical park. It however, was not. After losing Mike soon after the mid-innings interval, and Carl predictably following suit almost instantaneously for 49; still not quite having managed a Margate cricket club half century in his four years he been at the club; things were starting to sway towards the fortunes of Canterbury!

In what felt like a very slow saunter, we painstakingly crawled towards our target in the ten overs after drinks. Batting at six and still needing fifty to win from ten overs; I made my emphatic appearance at the crease! Batting in partnership with a new club member. I felt compelled to lead the charge towards our attainable target due to my now senior status at Margate! As it happened, even with my comprehensive attempts to successfully stroke the ball into gaps nicely at a run a ball pace, we unfortunately soon found ourselves needing 25 off the last three overs. I was either going to crunch a few match-winning boundaries and be the Polo Farm hero, or we were going to lose, and forever be immortalised as a batting bottler! Admittedly, to assist in my heroic endeavours, I did intentionally run out the new club member; due to his somewhat lacking cardio-vascular system! After all we still needed 20 to win off two overs! So, with Tom now at the crease with me; we had a shot!

With myself able to gain possession of the strike at the start of the penultimate over; it was now or never! This was the time I would get us close enough to take back the win that we should have had inevitably secured after our comprehensive start, or this was the time we would lose the game! Facing their returning opening bowler, whom by this point had now become considerably less effective due to a lacking amount of swing movement; I had to pick my area! So, just like in 2015 vs Littlebourne; cow corner was open! Was I going to target the gaping hole? Well — I tried! Utilising my vast wealth of previous experience from my prior failings four years earlier, I opted to only target 'moo town' if it was in my slot! As it happened, a visit to cow city never materialised, where I was forced to play a series of shots in reaction to where the bowler sent each delivery down. I'm pretty sure the bowler knew exactly what I was trying to do; keeping each ball so far outside my off stump, the only place I could accrue enough power to score an adequate number of runs was over extra cover! One ball on my stumps or just outside and it would have been curtains for Canterbury there and then; seeing the leather sailing over the agricultural boundary! I will give him his dues however, he bowled well and hence, all I could do was take a series of 2s and 3s on the offside to get us with striking distance for our final gambit in the last over!

With myself somehow getting back on strike after a well-run leg bye off the previous over's last ball, I was now facing a young off spin bowler. Tom and I both agreed that taking each run as it comes would be the best course of action to seeing us over the line. To my surprise, eight to win, quickly became four to win from five balls after a well-placed, and eloquent backward cut from myself. I initially only conceived a scampered two was on offer but the ball somehow trickled over the boundary! I thought, *"Yes! This is it, we can cruise from here!"* Oh, how I was wrong! After a dot and success in scoring one off the next ball; we consequently only required three from three balls! Then — tragedy struck! Tom caught a leading edge and spooned the ball back to the bowler! Fortunately, we were able to cross to get me back on strike!

Now needing three from two balls, it was just like the World Cup final! Lewis Fillary who had consequently just joined me at the crease must have been feeling the tension! Batting at number 11, he was propelled into playing the crucial supporting role of bearing the untold weight of the team! This next passage of play, I must admit, I have since rehearsed over and over again in my brain for the days and months after! Regrettably, I took the single to bring us within two off the last delivery, but by doing so, this put the young 15-year-old on strike; placing all the pressure on him! Lewis consequently missed the ball and was run out at the other end! We had lost by one run, and hence Margate were cast the undesirable role of New Zealand in this amateur dramatic reconstruction of that great final on the 14th of July!

I have perpetually thought about that moment since; I should have turned that single down to leave two to win off the last ball, and keep myself on strike? This however, would have been a risky tactic; knowing full well the unwelcome comments from the spectating team if we then had then lost by one run! I have since consoled myself in this convincing justification that it would have been too big of a risk to action! The off-hand comments of not being a team player would have been too big of a burden for even me to withstand as my amateur cricket career moves into a new decade. As it happened the game is now mostly forgotten to the sands of time and my reputation is still intact!

I actually only made 29 that day. One more run would have seen a tie. One more run from Carl would have also seen a tie, and also bring up his maiden fifty for the club! Oh well, all things happen for a reason and that day it wasn't supposed to be!

WATER-GATE (FINALLY REVENGE FOR EUROVISION!) - 2019

Now, for legal reasons, I must say at this point in the memoir, this has in no way anything to do with the controversy of the same name relating to the United States President; Richard Nixon! It just so happens that water is the catalyst for the somewhat unfortunate events!

Anyway, to bring you up to speed, in a weekend leading up to the World Cup final; Brett clearly had not learnt from his prior transgressions of four years prior when he knowingly agitating me at the Eurovision night! Before arriving at the ground at my usual early time to conduct the final pitch preparations. As always at home, I went through the ritualistic motions of my personally perceived compulsory pre-match morning routine. An early morning four-mile run; two pints of water in my Stella glass that was somewhat 'borrowed' from a pub; Mother making me my second coffee of the day; a salad bowl lunch, and finally, listening to the calming sounds of Mozart and Beethoven in the car whilst on transit to the game! Due to my ASD and the substantially meticulous nature of my brain; this habitual and unchanging schedule had to be obeyed for all 18 weeks of the league season! Consequently, if the routine ever becomes disturbed by any external 3rd party, all hell would break loose; resulting in a poor individual performance!

Having been successful on this Saturday in June to go through the said motions, I felt ready for the game against Boughton and Eastwell CC; my pitch looked like a decent deck (it wasn't), final prep had gone well, and I was in the right mindset to put in a performance. Unfortunately, putting the final touches to the pitch was where my day went from good; to bad; to awful. Upon walking the length of the ground with the sizeable yellow ten-litre jerry can in my right hand, I noticed that Billy had made his ever 'punctual' arrival to the game, having bought with him an assortment of little water pistols for his now four-year-old son; Dylan. Now, for those of you who don't know, getting sprayed with water when one is not supposed to get wet, for example anything that doesn't involve a shower or a swimming pool, I absolutely despise with great conviction! It is one of my four ASD triggers, the others being; someone sitting in my seat, ruining my set routines and purposefully knocking my head. When anyone intentionally decides to push one of those four buttons; I instantaneously turn into a metaphorical bull upon seeing a red rag; I simply flip! So, when Brett consciously hung this non-literal red rag in my face by straying water from one of these little water pistols, I — was kind enough to give him a warning shot; threw the large empty petrol can half-way towards the boundary from the edge of the square, and stormed off into the clubhouse to, funnily enough, get myself a pint of water!

Some time had now past, I somewhat calmed down and thought the whole situation had blown over. Oh, how I was wrong! Not initially sighting that water was still being squirted at people, I thought it'll be best to inspect the deck and provide my experienced thoughts on how the pitch would play. I think however, Brett, Dylan and co; picked up upon my hate of water on my dry self and continued their little folly of liberal water flinging! My blood was starting to boil! I understand that it probably appears that this is completely irrational, but think of fingers down a chalkboard; that is how it feels to me! Now, with myself somewhat lacking a great ability to verbally negotiate my way out of this antagonising circumstance; physical intervention was again my last resort! I had previously provided a warning shot, but now unfortunately for Brett, it was the time to act!

Being the only adult contributor of celebrating 'Josh Irritation Day'; I firstly attempted to sanction Brett for his premeditated actions; fruitlessly chasing him around the ground to no avail. I soon gave up, but young Dylan continued! Now clearly, I was not going to do to him what I had envisaged for Brett; nothing more than a jovial 'placing' on the ground was in store for Billy's son; however, Billy did not know this at the time! All he could see was that I was angry, and hence not quite sure of my intended actions. So, in a serious tone that never before have I heard directed at me; he shouted,

"Don't you fucking touch him or I'll smash your face in!"
I quite literally shat myself! Bill had never spoken to me like that; he has directed that tone to other people in my company yes, but not at me. Evidently, Bill was worried that I had not accounted for Dylan's age and thus wouldn't act accordingly, so I understand his reaction. Brett however, was fair game!

As a result of chasing Dylan, Brett was now standing near me as he thought he was safe and now out of the firing line. Oh, how the tide had now turned! Then on the same ground where Brett and I so famously witnessed the cricket week events with a bottle of fizz four years prior, proceeded to rugby dump tackle him onto the hard Astro pitch! This undoubtedly demonstrated my seriousness of messing with my autistic buttons, and I'm sure because of this, he will think twice in the future! Most importantly though, I finally had revenge for Eurovision! I finally, had shown some strength.

This did; however, result in Brett playing his final hand in our four-year-old game of figurative ASD poker; by claiming I had broken his phone via the competency of my rugby tackling skills, and that I needed to pay for the damage! Admittedly, there was a significant crack on the corner of his iPhone and hence sounded very convincing in his demands. The effect of Brett's trump card went on for a good ten minutes until I finally surrendered and admitted defeat, by caving into agreeing for the reimbursement of his somewhat urgent repair. He then proceeded to laugh hysterically and confess he had broken it weeks ago; he just wanted to see my reaction. I then couldn't do anything but nervously laugh in unison with him; after all, he is one of my best mates!

Clearly rattled by this whole palaver, I spent the next hour very quiet and reserved in my demeanour; objectively contrasting to my normal personality. It soon came to pass that we were batting first in the game, and that I was batting at three. Perhaps, I should have said that after the morning we've all had, I'd go down the order, but I didn't! Consequently, what happened next I needed like a hole in my head! Upon watching our openers tough it out in the early overs, I obtained yet another glass of water due to that day's scorching heat. Tom then proceeded to lose a game of odds to Billy and slapped this plastic glass full of water out of my hand; getting me even wetter in the process! I was furious but had no idea how to react! All I could do was sit out the spectating team circle; perfectly still and silent. Essentially, I was what one could recall as 'typically' ASD for a brief period of time.

Soon enough, Mike was dismissed, and it was my turn to bat. This is why I say I should have postponed my entry to the crease that day, as I was in no fit mental state to put a performance in; consequently scoring one off 18 balls. All I could think of was the previous events and how they had affected my short-term mental health. Inevitably, I soon found myself walking off the pitch; absolutely livid at my entire team! They knew what I'm like and how I react to specific situations; I was nothing but adamant that I was going to retire as of next week and never play again! As such, I soon found myself sitting in the car blaring my calming classical music from the beige Williamson Nissan Micra, A.K.A, 'The Granny Wagon'! I had it all; from Beethoven's '5th' to 'Pomp and Circumstance'! As far as Margate was concerned, I was done! What my team must have been thinking, I have absolutely no idea. But it was the only way I was going to return to the game after tea; I was actually a fraction away from driving home; effectively intending to abandon the game! But there probably would have been no coming back if I had changed my mind!

I sat there for a good half hour listening to this soothing music, all while the team were playing. To be honest, and probably egoistically, I couldn't really care less whether we were all out for 60 that day, or whether we had smashed 300 off 40 overs; I was not in a good place! From memory, we actually bowled Boughton out for sixty-odd and won the game! But the fact remains the same; don't press one of my four buttons! Brett subsequently, and most regrettably, started showing the signs of a bad hip following my thumping dump tackle. For that, I was sorry, I didn't intend to hurt Brett; I was more simply attempting to demonstrate my anger around the situation as I lack the ability to tell him when in that situation. I just hope when he reads this particular memoir, that finally after what has been effectively a four-year ASD cold war, that the Berlin wall has finally fallen, and that we have now found peace!

Needless to say, and by ending on a lighter note. As a result of this; whenever anyone needs to calm down amongst the cricket club membership, the phrase *"Do you need to listen to some classical music?"* typically rears it's ugly head!

CRAIG-GATE: BILL'S HOUSEWARMING - 2019

To continue this apparent trend of 2019 social controversies; this next memoir is situated at Bill's new home which he bought two weeks prior to these events. After another historic win against Nelson; completing the league double against them. Bill invited the team over to his new gaff to celebrate the conclusion of the necessary legal paperwork to enjoy an evening of cards against humanity, cricket highlights, and of course, copious amounts of alcohol!

In attendance that August evening were the usual suspects of obviously myself, Bill, Carl Taylor and Danielle; but additionally; Tom, Brett and Craig decided to make the effort for this momentous occasion! Having not eaten anything that day apart from a spot of tea between innings and my weekly M&S chicken and bacon salad bowl for lunch, I, to say the least, didn't have to drink too much for it to have a significant effect. After half a bottle of gin; a few rum and cokes and an entire bottle of red wine later; which the latter, was completely unbeknownst to me until after these events. It was decided by a certain 3rd party to take 'full' advantage of my self-inflicted state! Words cannot really describe the pickle I was in that evening. I suppose the best way to illustrate this to you, would be to reinforce the fact that as I am the proud owner of not only a 2:1 undergraduate degree but also a masters, I unsurprisingly hold a particular set of academic skills (with some support!); and even then, I lacked the mental capacity to orally recite the alphabet! Yes, evidently the only person to instigate the subsequent events could have only been Craig! Admittedly, I have been led to believe he was egged on by other people however, he was undeniably the main facilitator!

A,B,C?????

Even though I do not remember this next section happening, I certainly recall the end result! Craig saw it his evenings sole imperative that to gain entry into my phone and 'tinker' with the various aspects of it, would be a highly amusing and comical thing to do. The only part personally remembered by me is that I did actually provide my unlocked phone to Craig earlier in the night as he wanted to help a single fellow cricketer out by 'pimping up' one's Tinder profile. To clarify, I don't actually use this social platform seriously, I use it more crudely for the sole purpose of collecting matches with the opposite sex to see how many girls fancy a bit of autistic Josh! From memory, he did do a good job which has instigated many hilarious conversations with these females; the majority starting along the political lines of Brexit and my staunch advocation for it!

Anyway, this makeover of one's flippant online dating profile reached its conclusion within a matter of minutes, and I soon had the phone back in my safe and secure possession. Following this, I believe I was ushered to Billy and Danielle's bed at around midnight. With the party still flowing nicely, after an hour of being asleep, Craig clearly saw great potential in the unlocked contents of my phone and made great strides in his attempt for round two! I must confess, his method in how he was able to commence round two was very clever. So, clearly with myself not even knowing my own name by this point, let alone recalling the universally agreed ordering of the alphabet; Craig utilised this for his own self-gain! He proceeded to pull the phone out of my pocket and conjure up some farfetched indoctrination that he required immediate access to my phone! All in the hope that I would consequently punch in my access code to essentially hand my entire life on a plate! And oh boy! Did he have a banquet!

Craig apparently came screeching back into Bill's new living room in sheer joy and elation that his cunning scheme had actually worked; paraphrasing,

> *"I've got Josh's phone! I've got Josh's phone! What should I do with it?!!?"*

As it happened, what didn't Craig do with it? He firstly re-familiarised himself with my Tinder profile; messaging the remaining 71 of my well-earned matches! He changed my Facebook profile picture to a man standing outside parliament proudly holding up a 'remain in the EU' banner, and subsequently renewed my current status on the social media platform to, *"So glad I voted remain!"* Although, this was actually quite funny, he then also messaged my Sunday team group chat; Herne CC, that I was going to smash an emphatic 100 off 300 balls that afternoon! He then coerced Danielle into taking a picture of himself, Billy, Brett, Carl and Tom in the middle of the living room. And needed little encouragement from Billy to change the lovely wallpaper of my cricket square at Margate, to a graphic and realistic representation of two homosexual men sodomise each other. And finally, and probably most infuriatingly; attempted to mask the fact he was the primary antagonist of these actions and replaced my phone where I had left it; in my pocket.

The Phone Fabricators and their Ring Leader

I woke up at 5:30am that Sunday morning, where I was greeted to Bill, Carl and Danielle still awake from the previous night's exploits. Most probably because the engaged couple were actually unable to retire to their sleeping quarters, as they had a comatose inhabitant in their bed for the majority of the night! Anyway, I woke up; expecting Dad to pick me up at 9am that morning. Having been welcomed to the sight of the trio still playing 'Cards against Humanity' and, yes, still drinking. I thought it'll be best that because my situation couldn't get any worse and having already agreed to play cricket at 1pm for Herne; that to continue my drinking endeavours would be the wisest thing to do! So, there we were playing the game while still drinking, where I was soon told to look at my phone. Apart from obviously seeing the newly applied wallpaper of two young males sexually gratifying each other, I didn't immediately notice anything else at first. I knew however, something wasn't quite right! They then told me to go on to Tinder; I evidently saw what he did with the 71 matches and laughed. Now slightly worried by this point as to what else had happened, they then directed me to Facebook; I couldn't find the app! I then looked for WhatsApp and Facebook Messenger; couldn't find those either! The little five-foot-seven fucker had not only replaced the phone in my pocket to delay the discovery of his actions, but had also deleted the apps he meddled with to delay my inspection! I found everything that he had done! I was furious!

To be honest, this day couldn't have started much worse. Where I then had the bomb shell revelation that I also had to face the repercussions of his doings when playing for Herne. I had it in the ear all game as clearly I didn't make 100 off 300 balls! I was still drunk at the start! So, what did I score? I scored 3 off 59 balls; I couldn't even get myself out I was that inebriated! I then attempted to forget about the issues and re-download WhatsApp and Facebook Messenger when I got home; which only resulted in me trying to find the said applications every time I went back on to the phone in the three hours leading up to Dad collecting me. After the third or fourth time of repeating this failed scout for apps; I was ready to flip! Because someone, A.K.A, 'Craig', had the audacity to rearrange the order of my phone and essentially delete the structure of my daily routines. I, in addition to screaming at the top of my lungs at 6am in a quiet little culs-de-sac, proceeded to throw my phone at full velocity into Billy's new sofa and watch it crash on to the wooden floor with a huge thud!

In what felt like slow motion, the phone landed on its front! I was expecting the worst! Everyone was expecting the worst. How it didn't break; I'll never know! But it survived — or so I thought. Two days later on my walk to the gym, I noticed my wireless headphones weren't connecting to the phone and allow me to play music. Although I thought the phone survived that little ordeal; I had actually broken the Bluetooth antenna! What was I going to do? Well, in fits of rage at Craig, I stormed off to my phone provider and unconvincingly attested to the fact I had never dropped my phone, let alone knowingly treat it like a pebble at the beach! As the screen was undamaged, they swiftly took it away and gave me a reconditioned phone a week later! That phone however, was also broken and eventually conceded after three weeks and gave me a brand new iPhone!

So Josh, what did you get out of that evening I hear you ask? What was your prize for the night? What was the moral of the story? Have you learnt your lesson? Well, my prize was the intermittent use a much older and slower iPhone 5S for the majority of September. My lesson learnt was that screaming at the top of my lungs in a quiet culs-de-sac at 6am in the morning will lead to external remarks. These comments specifically coming from Billy's nan who lives one road across from him. Yes readers; Billy, Carl and Danielle were not the only ones to experience my little meltdown 1st hand that morning; Bill's nan also got the great honour of hearing me shout profane expletives at 6am on that ill-fated Sunday morning! And yes, I don't think she was too pleased!

The Great Mexican Stand-Off - 2019

As we near the end of this catalogue of stories from my cricketing life; this next short tale comes in the form of the penultimate league game of our 2019 campaign. Up against our friends at Worth CC; this was the moment that will shape the future of my amateur career as we move into the next decade!

After two controversial dismissals in the previous fortnight; this game was where my goose was well and truly cooked! Batting first and after a strong start of 50-0 after ten overs, we quickly lost two wickets in the space of three balls, where I found myself at the crease with the scoreboard now 50-2. Having not been able to buy a run the previous two games; I was somewhat nervous for this next at-bat. This was probably compacted with Billy now figuratively breathing up my neck for the Margate batting award; only 26 runs behind! So, there I was, asking our umpire for my usual guard of leg and prepared to face my first ball. I lined it up nicely and got in behind it well for a convincing dot. This is however, where the story takes one large and abrupt U-turn!

With Worth's young wicketkeeper standing in no man's land; five-foot back. I positioned my stance one foot outside the popping crease; the bowler proceeded to deliver a pitched up, floaty out swinger on a 5th stump line. Evidently, not wanting to give up this opportunity to get off the mark, I produced this huge waft at the ball, but instead of hitting the ball, I only made connection with the air we all breathe; and watched the ball follow nicely through to the youthful gloveman! The keeper, who obviously sighted my positioning at the crease, utilised this and quickly attempted to stump me, or shall I say run out, from five yards back. Using my own knowledge and experience of wicketkeeping, I foresaw his inevitable intention and promptly, in my opinion, just about moved the willow across the popping crease simultaneously as the ball hit the stumps.

Well — this is what I thought. With our own 15-year-old fast bowler standing at square leg officiating the game, he had not quite yet learnt how to read the game and know when to bend the rules if the situation calls for it. Consequently, as it was such a close call, he thought it was out, and gave it as such! With myself knowing full well who was umpiring; knowing I was actually in as I watched the ball hit the stumps when the bat crossed the line; and being fully aware that it was so close. Worth would not have complained if the decision didn't go their way. The young lad; however, insisted upon his ardent line that it was out!

Unsurprisingly, I stood my ground; persistently citing my firm opinion that I was in. He continued with his ill-judged decision;

whereby Worth at this point were already in their celebration circle! I however, wasn't going anywhere just yet! The young square leg umpire subsequently made moves to confer with our standing umpire; with myself still standing my ground at the striking end. As far as I was concerned, the wrong decision was taken and consequently I perpetually continued my stand-off for must have been a good four minutes! Quite literally, I was like Jordan Belfort in the film 'Wolf of Wall Street; *"I was not fucking leaving!"*

This little altercation did have one upside however, it was a good job this happened if for the only reason that because by the point the young umpire gave his initial decision, Billy was only just pulling up his whites! Let alone anywhere near ready to occupy the crease with his pads on and bat in hand! Brett happened to still be in the changing room removing his pads when he was called by the team due to my persistence in the matter. He had just about crossed the boundary line on to the outfield when John agreed with our young lad and ominously raised his index finger. I had to wave the white flag on this Mexican stand-off; the figurative sombrero had to be removed; I had to surrender! There was no more fighting on the beaches that August afternoon. So, just like the French in World War Two, I was forced to accept my fate; I had to put up with the direct occupation of the stringent rule of cricket Nazis'!

I do accept that our young bowler wanted to adhere to the laws of cricket, and obviously felt I was out. However, I still to this day attest to my bat being across that line when the ball made contact! That said, the young lad has to learn somewhere, just hopefully next time, he'll use this experience and read the game situation after we had already lost two wickets in the same over! As it happened, we were bowled out for 120 that day after I was incorrectly given out. Anyway, Billy went on to make 20 and in turn put himself only six runs behind me going into the last game for the honours of lifting the 2019 batting award; but that story is still to come!

WE'RE FAMOUS! - 2019

On bank holiday Monday of 2019, I was able to secure quite a special and novel game of cricket for Margate cricket club; an away day vs Sanderstead CC in Surry. Now, I can hear you all thinking, it's just like any old game isn't it? Well — no. This game was filmed for the purpose to be uploaded on to YouTube for their plus 11 thousand subscribers to watch! What a day we had! Made even better by the reaction when our young fast bowler found out we were playing them! Apparently, he watches all their games every weekend! So let's just say he was 'a little' star struck that he was physically playing the faces of his Sunday morning viewing!

Being scorching hot that day, we unfortunately lost the toss and were subjected to the delights of fielding first. With me firstly electing to don the gloves for the first ten overs just in case I had a shocker with the bat. I didn't do myself any disservice; notching up yet another sharp stumping to my ever-growing career collection. So at least when I passed possession of the gloves to Jake, I had at the very worst shown to the internet cricket community I could play cricket! This all obviously wasn't before we introduced ourselves to Sanderstead before the start of the game. Now, clearly seeing that this is quite a popular and well-known team within cricket circles, this old chap wrongly assumed I knew who he was! After shaking hands with Dan who commentates and edits the videos, he proceeded to point out a few of their more 'familiar' faces. This ageing player then expectantly came up to me, where I quote,

"Oh you know who I am don't you?"

I didn't have the foggiest idea! So, instead of awkwardly agreeing with him as per what social convention dictates. I proceeded to tersely reply,

"Errrm, no. Who are you?"

Everyone within earshot was in hysterics, the player embarrassingly turned around and proceeded to forget the whole thing ever happened! The man later revealed to me he was called 'Derek', where I believe I ran him out to top off the whole palaver! Of course it was unintentional to firmly put this chap in his place; it's just typical Josh speaking his mind! It did however, set the game up for a light-hearted affair though!

That Stumping!

Anyway, back to the cricket. Thinking we had Sanderstead's number; having them sixty-odd for four, we unilaterally agreed that to bring myself and Malcolm on to bowl would be the kindest thing to do, after all, we didn't want to chase a hundred and finish by 5pm; which wouldn't have made for good viewing! So, there I was bowling my pies, where the first few balls were ok; even castling their number three after a vicious; loopy full toss that should have been put in the adjacent field for six! I probably should have taken myself off after that great high, a that was the end of my bowling success; where I quote *"A fielding exhibition"* was still to come.

The Full-Toss Wicket!

With Brett now bowling, he proceeded to loop up six consecutive deliveries outside this right-hander's off stump. So, what did he do? Well — he hit every single ball in the over right at me with a great amount of velocity at cover! The first; I shielded away like a little girl! The second; I produced an unconvincing half stop. The third; found its way into my cupped hands; followed immediately with an ironic Cristiano Ronaldo like celebration! The fourth; the Margate mole made an unwelcome appearance as the ball popped up towards my private parts! The fifth; the 'fielding exhibition', where I sharply ran to my left, put in a one-handed dive, successfully collected the ball and attempted to throw down the stumps for an unlikely run out! Dan the cameraman and his nearby colleagues were fits of applause! Where I was additionally attributed the considerable compliment that it was 'the finest display of fielding he had on camera!' Finally, the sixth; a mirror to the first; a pitiful half stop, which was palmed off to Jamie at long-off! Honestly, give it a watch yourself, if you've taken the time to get this far in the book, it's worth an extra half an hour of your life!

https://www.youtube.com/watch?v=OQCX3a-gVog&list=WL
(The link to the game)

With my fielding exploits now out the way, it was time to bring on my brother Chris, A.K.A, 'The Margate Murali'! A name coined by the opposition by his, somewhat 'suspect' bowling action! Chris, to put it bluntly, hadn't played a game of cricket since 2006, but he filled in for us after a last-minute drop out. He did however; get a wicket, so I think he enjoyed the day!

The Fielding Exhibition

Anyway, with the fielding section now concluded and Sanderstead back in the game after our gifting of many, many runs; it was our turn to bat. This was not before tea and copious amounts of cakes, sandwiches and brownies! Unfortunately for us, it wasn't a great start for Margate; finding ourselves one hundred-odd for four when I reached the crease. With myself still hungover from our family picnic the previous day, I couldn't do anything but make a fool out of myself! I didn't even make a run that day, but boy did I get done like a kipper to dismiss me. The same batsman who elected to bombard me with all six balls in one over, only needed four balls of his right-angling leg spin to see an inevitable reward! Ball one was a leg-spinner; a convincing leave followed. Ball two was a leg-spinner again which resulted in a thick edge that just about fell short of 1st slip. Ball three; yet another leg-spinner; an unconvincing swipe across the line this time! Ball four; to be honest, I should have seen it coming, but it was a slider that went straight on; making me look like an inept batsman for all the internet to see! Have a look down the comments on the video, it's not particularly pretty viewing! My downfall was the start of the domino effect; seeing only a couple of futile cameos from Carl Taylor and Chris, whom yes readers, hadn't played for 13 years and scored more runs than me!

But nonetheless, it was a brilliant day! Great fun was had by all; all topped off with a joint fines circle between Margate and Sanderstead with a BBQ and free beer! It just so happened that after all the banter I was dishing out to Carl before the game as to who would feature in a short Facebook video meme, that it would be me who featured as the viral internet sensation from the game!

The Forward Defence...again!

First Play and Miss...

Second Play and Miss...

And...I'm Out!

THE BATTING RETIREMENT - 2019

It is as we transition past the dying embers of the 2019 cricket season and into the dull and grey winter months. That at this age of 25, I have concluded that a retirement of batting in the top order is probably the safest move for not only the team and the club, but my own individual well-being on and off the field. This might seem like an odd decision for any unsuspecting 3rd party seeing that I am still the right side of 30; however, please allow this final memoir, as it currently stands, to elaborate further upon this carefully considered and difficult decision.

Although it must be acknowledged that this year, without the ties of a cricket loathing girlfriend and the unshackled quantity of time a Masters by Research facilitated; I had a good start to the 2019 season; even leading the clubs 'most runs list' for 17 out of the 18 league games. It is at this juncture in my cricketing career that the figurative camel's back was well and truly broken! In the three matches leading up to the final game which was against St Margaret's, it appeared that I could not accept that I was dismissed. I not only once, not twice, but in all three games stood my ground attesting to my perception that a poor umpiring decision had been made, culminating in the Mexican stand-off fiasco at Worth! It is at this point before the final game vs St Margaret's, that in an amalgamation of this and the undue stress it has caused, that I announced this would be my final venture batting in the lofty heights of Margate cricket club's top five.

With only a six-run lead over Bill in the whole season tally going into this final league fixture; all was to play for! After an initial squabble as to who would open the batting, it was agreed that because on paper he should be the victor in an arm wrestle, that this would be the easiest and fairest way of settling the significant disagreement. So, after demolishing a heaped plate of tea, mainly consisting of carbohydrates, we beared arms and began the contest! It was a well-fought affair, with an unsuspecting ebb and flow that sharply took Bill by surprise. Although initially, he seized the upper hand in the opening moments, with the sheer will and desire to win; I pushed back his opening salvo and forced him into playing the endurance game! Eventually, Billy's ailing wrist caved in; resulting in a deafening 'click!'. I had won, and with it, the honour of allowing Bill to set the score by opening. The game within a game had officially commenced!

It wasn't a confident start for ol' Billy Bobs; playing and missing at many of the opening deliveries. Clearly, nerves were starting to show for my close-trailing teammate, it surely wasn't going to be long before he nicked off and set a low target for me batting at three. In what must have been a slow and agonising experience for him, one run slowly became two, and two, distressingly for me, transitioned into six with a well-struck boundary. With that hefty crunch through the covers he also had a tie for the lead! I now was forced to score some runs when I batted. Clearly, that metaphorical feeling of dread once residing firmly on Bill's back, had unceremoniously sold-up shop and moved to a new dwelling on my broad shoulders! I must also admit, even though Billy scoring runs was clearly of benefit to our run chase as a team and undoubtedly was enjoyed by most players, I wished for nothing other than an early demise for him! Self-admittedly however, if Billy was in my situation, he would be thinking the same! With Carl now strolling off the field after providing some untimely catching practice for the opposition, I now found myself heading in the opposite direction!

Knowing this was to be my final knock in the top order, everyone was clearly thinking that a recreation of Alistair Cook's famous last innings at the Oval was all but guaranteed. That, however, did not happen. Taking as much time as humanly possible before commencing my final gambit, I eventually punched gloves with Bill, called him a twat, and asked for my all too familiar leg guard. What happened next, would be impossible to script, where one could only watch as the events unfolded. Evidently, with this so-called uninvited resident of the 'unconvincing start' now squatting on my broad shoulders, this only spurred William in batting me into submission! After accumulating a few singles via a number of edges and light pushes, this is where Bill went bang! Before I knew it, he was not just a gettable six runs ahead of me, he was now 20 in front, after firing 14 from the shite and temping off-spinner. The only words I could verbalise were,

"You're gonna' make me get a score now aren't you?"

To which he instantaneously replied *"Yup!"* So, with Brett, Craig, Carl and the Sedgewicks keeping a close tally of mine and Billy's individual totals; on what can only be described as a rotting blue coloured pallet designed for crated goods. It supported the presentation of my perpetually static score, and Billy's increasingly growing lead! To be frank, this attentive update on our current totals probably didn't help my attempt that day to win the batting award! However, there was nothing I could do as the game swiftly progressed!

It was at this crossroads where the poor umpiring decisions that haunted the second half of my 2019 season, had one last cruel and sadistic trick up its sleeve! This came in the form of the opposition umpire not giving Billy out lbw. This slow, non-spinning, off-spinner produced a delivery pitching on what could have only been one-foot in-front of the popping crease in line with the middle peg, all while striking Bill's back leg while his knee was planted firmly on the Durban like Tivoli pitch! A huge appeal erupted from the 11 opposing players'; it was about as out as nicking off to second slip! A silent appeal consequently omitted from my struggling head; not mentioning my wry smile of impending relieve! Even Bill thought he was a goner! I thought my luck was finally in! To be honest, even Brett from the boundary couldn't come to any other conclusion than an early shower and nervous wait for William! The umpire pondered his decision for a subjectively endless period of time, eventually uttering a sentence that still gives me nightmares, even now!

"No, not out, going over the top and miles down leg".
Billy couldn't believe his luck; it was hitting middle of middle! With himself only on 30 and consequently only an attainable 20 in-front of me; I was essentially in the process of evicting that most unwelcome metaphorical occupant; this simply could not be happening!

Billy went on to make 51 that day, and in the process, set a lofty personal target. When his dismissal eventually materialised, even though he didn't actually say it; with myself only on ten at the time, he must have been thinking *"Yup, that'll be enough"*. I don't need to say this, but it was. I closely followed my batting award opponent after practising a poorly rehearsed strictly come dancing routine and was abruptly stumped. The contest was over, the 2019 season was now over, and with it, so was my membership of batting in the top five! I knew exactly what was going to come next, it manifested itself in the sight and sound of that now infamous, unforgettable and bellowing cackle.

"HAHAHAHAHA, I am the King! Bow to your Master! All hail King Billy!"

He effectively began a coronation that only he attended; walking around the ground placing pretend crowns on his own head! While I was there, essentially lying in wake at my own batting funeral, nothing could provide enough solace for this degenerated 'second-placer'. So many years I've come second in the batting award, and this year, tragically, would be no different. All I could do was agonisingly walk to the changing room with the loud background undertones of Bill 'modestly', relishing his comeback win; put my jeans on; grab myself a beer, and watch the remainder of the game reach an inevitable completion.

So, I conclude volume one of my memoirs on this rather pertinent and somewhat melancholy note. What the future may bring, who knows? With Sam finally back in the fold and committed for the 2020 season; we may even witness a return of my junior bowling glory days. Perhaps even a revival of that once all too familiar scorebook occurrence of 'stumped; Winch, bowled; Williamson' — maybe? Only time will tell. But, with my eyesight now not what it was; where additionally I no longer possess the batting power and brute force I, so emphatically displayed in my obese youth; and my utter reluctance to accept a wrong umpiring decision when batting high in the order. That I must take stock of this moment, accept my fate, and move forward into the next decade with a refreshed vigour of batting in the lower order at six or seven and with it, a new team-orientated purpose as a running specialist in the latter overs! However, if I'm being honest, that is probably only supplementary to my primary purpose for playing next year and beyond; the social!

EPILOGUE

I firstly would like to thank you for reaching the end of what has been an absolute pleasure to write. I hope you enjoyed reading essentially what was the equivalent of the - 'This is your life of Josh Williamson'. My favourite stories by far were the strip club and Liverpool is at home memoir! The Zak Crawley one is up there too!

At the time of finishing this first volume, it is November of 2019. Although, admittedly, my top order batting days are behind me, there will inevitably be more cricket stories to reminisce upon in the near and distant future. I will make it known here that at the end of this first volume, that if you have enjoyed my life thus far; please set a date in your diary for five years' time! I plan to release volume two as I pass the age of 30 in 2024. So, bear with me, have trust that my future life in the sport will be as eventful and action-packed as the first 16 years; where I hope that by reading this series of memoirs it can inspire any other autistic person to do the same and live life to the fullest!

So, I say thank you! Thank you for your patience! Thank you for enjoying my life! And finally, thank you for supporting me!

QUOTES AND ACKNOWLEDGEMENTS

"Cricket. It's made me who I am"

"All things happen for a reason"

I would like to thank all those involved in the formation of these life events and for agreeing to be mentioned in the book. Firstly, to Margate cricket club for everything you have given me to play this great game. To initially Ian Dovey for being so accommodating in the very early years. Then subsequently; Ian Robinson, who gave me that vote of confidence all those years ago; selecting my ten-year-old self to play for the Thanet under 10's in 2004, and consequently nurturing me on and off the field though the entire junior game into adult cricket.

On a social level, I would like to give a huge thank you to a few special mentions. One to Billy Woollard and Brett Kirk who were both with me along the ride for all of chapter four; for their understanding of my issues and shielding me from the vast majority of consequences following many of my social mishaps. Another to Dan Carter who seemed to have the unnerving tendency to be present for most of the important bits. A thank you to Carl Taylor, who is the most recent of close mates to join my small circle of best friends, but by no means is any less significant.

And finally, a special mention for my parents, my nan, grandad and grandpa. All of you supported me in those difficult formative years of growing up, enabling me to do whatever I took an interest in and allow me to play the sport that had given me so much. Nan and Grandad who both willingly and enthusiastically watched me play in not only the sunshine, but in the cold and rain. Dad, who has scored virtually every game I've ever played, who has been with me with most of my cricketing triumphs, (apart from my first hundred!), but nevertheless unconditionally wielded those fine-tip coloured pens or iPad and suffered hours upon hours of my batting exploits. And finally, my mum, who drove me an unquantifiable amount of miles all over the county, supported me with all my issues relating to ASD, and for endlessly preparing the all-important teas in my adult years!

To conclude this rather self-indulgent and long-winded spiel, to describe what you have read, while also providing a homage to all the significant personalities in it. Without cricket and the friends I've made through playing this game, I fundamentally do not know where I would be in life.

"Why are you so wet?"